I0142444

Quantum Prayer

What Today's Science May Teach Us About the God Who Answers Prayer

By Gerald Baron

EDENSVEIL

Copyright © 2014 Gerald R. Baron
All rights reserved. Published in the United States by
EdensVeil Media
1319 Cornwall Ave.
Suite 200
Bellingham, Washington, 98225.
Originally published August, 2014. Edition 1.0

Table of Contents

About the Author

Gerald Baron is a writer/artist/entrepreneur but mostly a family man. While his career and interests have taken varied paths, his passion to understand what is true and real has never altered or diminished. This book is one result of that near-continuous study. Reflecting his varied interests he has written several other books including *Now Is Too Late: Survival in an Era of Instant News* called the best guide to crisis communication in the digital era. His book on developing relationships in business, *Friendship Marketing*, was published in 1997. In 2009 his book *A Fighter Pilot in Buchenwald: the Joe Moser Story* was published and led to a companion award-winning documentary called *Lost Airmen of Buchenwald* which he co-wrote and served as Executive Producer. He also wrote a guide to crisis communication planning called *OnePage Crisis Communication Playbook.*

His professional career has also been varied including four years as a university professor and the founder or co-founder of several successful companies including a software company, marketing and public relations firm, a regional magazine publishing company and a crisis communication technology firm. While not exactly a career, he also has a life long interest in art, painting and the study of aesthetics. His oil paintings are exhibited and sold at several locations including Skagit Valley, Washington and Palm Desert, California.

He attended Calvin College in Grand Rapids, Michigan and received a B.A. in Art and Speech Communications (Drama Emphasis) from Seattle Pacific University. He also earned an M.A. degree in Communications from Wheaton College and was granted an honorary doctorate from Trinity Western University in Langley, British Columbia.

He makes his home near the tiny town of Edison, Washington in rural Skagit County which served as home and inspiration for the well known artists of the Northwest School. He and his wife of forty-one years, Lynne, an accomplished interior and event designer, live at Carriage Hill Farm which also serves as the studio gallery for both artist and designer. They have three grown children and nine grandchildren, all living in northwest Washington state.

Introduction

I'm not a scientist, but I do pray. And sometimes, most of the time actually, I believe that there is Someone who hears me, who cares and who will even attend to my prayers in some mysterious way.

I'm also a rationalist and skeptic by nature. I want to know the truth. When it comes to prayer, I want to know if there is any coherent way of thinking about reality that can lead me to a rational conclusion that there really is a God who listens, cares and sometimes even answers.

As the first chapter asserts, most of us pray. According to Pew Research in 2012, only nine percent of Americans disavowed belief in God or a universal spirit. Presumably, the 90% plus who are self-proclaimed believers pray at least some of the time. Some, perhaps quite a few, like me wonder about its efficacy and wonder about to whom they are really addressing their petitions and expressions of gratitude and wonder. If you are one of those, then you might find my personal exploration of that question interesting -- perhaps even helpful to you. If you are one of those who will dismiss this question immediately with "take it on faith," or "science allows for no such possibility" then you may be disappointed. I encourage you to give it a try anyway. You might be surprised.

As a non-scientist I find fascinating what those on the front lines of our search for knowledge of the natural world have to teach us. Coming out of the "dark ages" of exploration of truth when we sought it primarily in our own souls and experiences, into the "enlightenment" of the search for truth in the natural world, we first discovered that there was remarkable order. We found the world predictable, understandable and perhaps even deterministic. This was a world that obeyed the strictest rules of a machine which for many obviated a need for "the God

5

hypothesis." But that changed. Beginning in the first quarter of the twentieth century we discovered a distinct uncertainty and lack of predictability in our world. The discoveries of this chaos and uncertainty have, strangely, contributed greatly to our expansion of technology. And while enlightenment science tended to disconnect the search for physical truth and spiritual reality, the opposite is happening as we will see in these pages.

There is no question that many ardent defenders of the naturalist explanation for reality and truth are venturing far beyond the realm of science when they declare that science explains away God and spiritual reality. Atheist philosopher Thomas Nagel in *Mind and Cosmos* succinctly described our current cultural situation regarding science and faith:

"In the present climate of a dominant scientific naturalism, heavily dependent on speculative Darwinian explanations of practically everything, and armed to the teeth against attacks from religion..."

While some scientists make overly ambitious claims for a scientific basis for destruction of belief, science itself does no such thing. At the same time, ardent defenders of traditional conservative Christian orthodoxy with an extreme literalist translation of ancient scripture are quick to dismiss any finding of science that contradicts firmly established ideas about reality. I am convinced, however, that thinking people coming from either worldview can find common ground on the most basic questions of truth, science and belief. That conviction lies at the heart of this personal exploration into what is true and coherent about science and faith.

As the last chapter will show, the journey into the fascinating world of science has profoundly affected my own thinking about the biggest questions. About who we are, where we came from, how we are to live, and what our destiny is. The most surprising thing, and possibly most profound discovery, is that contemporary science seems to leave plenty of room for God to act, to be involved, to exercise personal and universal providence, and even answer prayer. And he can do that without "intervening" in the fixed laws of nature, without resorting to the spectacular miracle.

I will not bother with a long list of thank yous. There are friends and family members who have contributed much to this through interesting discussion: Uncle Henry, Bill, Mike, Victor, Steve and James to name a few. Special thanks to James Bradley, retired professor of math from Calvin College who won a Templeton Foundation grant to study how randomness in the universe interacts with divine providence. Professor Bradley graciously gave much time in reviewing my non-professional explanations and musings. But let me be clear: errors are mine alone, especially where I resisted his caution related to the important topic of observation and consciousness. My parents and particularly my dad always encouraged a spirited inquiry into the biggest issues and demonstrated his own participation in that. Our three grown children, Chris, Geoff and Ashley and their spouses, have all made life more than interesting and their own inquiries into the depths of belief and reality have spurred me on. But my main acknowledgement goes to my wife, Lynne, who patiently puts up with my ramblings, my scary diversions of thought and contributes her own often perplexing questions on the reality of faith and life.

Chapter 1 Dissonance: Of Two Minds

Nearly everyone prays. I say nearly because while I believe in truth that everyone prays I cannot prove it. And there are some who are so adamant that they don't that while I don't believe them, I won't push it. What is remarkable about all that praying is that it takes place in a world where the inhabitants have for the past two hundred years largely accepted that no one is listening.

The big shift started with the "Enlightenment" which was a slow but certain adjustment in thinking about our world, God, and our place in it. Two of the primary markers in the dramatic shift in thinking were the discovery by Isaac Newton of the laws of the motion of the planets, otherwise known as the law of gravity, and the other was the publication of Origin of the Species by Charles Darwin. These didn't start the ball rolling toward a view of the world I will call "naturalism" but these did provide the intellectual support for those leading thinkers who were already viewing that God had been chased from his throne in the universe. Not only was he replaced on the throne by the deification of humans, but he was relegated to the dustbin of history in the new thinking.

The primary engines that drive our culture—media, entertainment, education, politics—are driven almost exclusively by those who believe that naturalism rules. Indeed, it is hard to ascend to the highest levels in these areas of endeavor without holding to the correct views on this important issue. They may not actually believe in naturalism and all it teaches, but they have to pretend that they do when performing their duties. This is in sharp contrast to how the majority of, at least, Americans continue to think. So we need to understand how this gap may have come about. While some scientists have rather sharply veered away from some of the underlying ideas of naturalism such as mechanism, reductionism and determinism, the ideas so heavily promoted for so long still are an underpinning of our culture. We are "spiritual" heirs of that French naturalist Laplace who was an early teacher of naturalism. The story goes that when asked by Napoleon about the role of God in the natural order of things, Laplace famously replied, "I have no need for that theory." While the interchange is likely fictional, it concisely explains naturalism and its early historical beginnings.

Naturalism, as I am defining it, is simply the idea that God is not necessary in the world in which we live. The fundamental idea is that our world and everything in it consist of substances and forces which can be measured and experienced; since God has not yet shown him or herself to be a substance or a force yielding to measurement, there is no need for that theory. Naturalism, due to the incredible power of science to unmask deep mysteries and generate useful products, teaches that everything can be explained without reference to God. Newton, Copernicus and Galileo showed that the sun "rose" because of the motion of the earth relative to the sun. This is quite different from the Greeks, who early on saw the sun as a god named Helios who rode his chariot across the skies. And different from the ancient Hebrews and their spiritual children, the Christians and Muslims, who believed that it was the Creator God Elohim who made his sun to shine on the righteous and the wicked alike. We now "know" of course that the earth moves around the sun in a highly predictable orbit completely controlled by the laws of physics and most specifically by the force of gravity. There is no need for gods named Helios or Elohim in this picture. When it comes to the rising and setting of the sun, we are all naturalists.

We adopted naturalism as a cultural value when it was demonstrated over time that it revealed a true picture of our world and could improve our lives. The simple acceptance that God was the cause behind everything we couldn't understand was seen, rightfully, by our intellectual leaders as a potential hindrance to knowledge. Knowledge was power and more importantly, control over our environment and our lives. But the intellectual leaders in the 1700s saw that a blind acceptance of God as an unquestioned and unquestionable answer to all mysteries hindered the curiosity and search for truth needed to better understand nature and gain control over our world and lives.

Take polio, for example. Early in the 1900s it was one of the most dreaded diseases with hundreds of thousands of pathetic victims around the world. I had relatives who were victims of polio. A man we called Uncle Lawrence went through life with a withered arm and hand. Parents prayed that their children would not be affected. The cause was unknown and it was in God's hand whether a child would be left paralyzed or killed by the disease. If scientists or researchers at the time had taken the anti-naturalism view that some things cannot be known and are in the hands of God, the prevention of it would be left to prayer. But they didn't. By this time, in 1909, the idea that there were natural causes for natural events was deeply embedded in the scientific community. We had come to see that if the cause could be determined, there might be a way found to deal with the cause and even prevent the disease. In 1909, a professor of pathology at the University of Vienna identified the poliovirus. That discovery led to the creation of vaccines by Jonas Salk in 1952 and Albert Sabin in 1962. Thanks to widespread vaccination by health authorities the number of cases of polio today numbers is in the low thousands. It is estimated that the discovery of the poliovirus by Dr. Landsteiner has saved hundreds of millions if not a billion plus lives. Polio eradication around the world is nearly in our grasp.

We are all naturalists now to at least some degree. We all believe that the world is highly predictable, that it conforms to discoverable laws and physical processes and that discovering these laws leads to knowledge and technological innovation that can make our world a better place. We are also aware, of course, that there is a dark side to this knowledge—born out by the most devastating wars and the greatest damage to our native earth that our brief story of life on this planet has seen.

But we are naturalists who pray. And that strange phenomenon is what this book is all about. How can we simultaneously believe in a senseless, heartless machine of which we are one infinitesimal and ultimately meaningless part, and still believe that there is an intelligence, a will, a divine purpose that is active and alive in our world? I was quite surprised to see several different studies, including one reported by Francis Collins in his book *The Language of God*, that showed that many, if not most, professional scientists are also "believers" in the sense that they believe in a God who answers prayer. This is truly remarkable. It is remarkable enough that study after study shows that well over 75% of people in the United States believe in God, in heaven and in prayer. But to have scientists, whose very foundation of thinking is based on the idea that all must be reduced to laws in order to discover truth, also believe in a God who answers prayer is really quite stunning. Maybe even more surprising is that younger scientists are more likely to be theists than older scientists.

At its simplest level I would attribute this apparent dissonance to the fundamental intuition that we all share. Despite over 200 years of the successful promotion of naturalism as the underlying foundation of our world and the resulting benefits, most still believe that there is Someone behind it all. That belief and intuition is captured in our very language. Naturalism implies a machine and that's the way the mechanistic view of the universe conceives it. Nature is a vast, self-perpetuating machine operated by the strictest of laws and forces. A machine that is finely-tuned, exquisitely balanced and is almost endlessly fruitful with the capability of creating and destroying life. But it is a machine and everyone instinctively knows that if there is a machine, there is a machinist. It is in actuality quite difficult to avoid this basic and simple intuition. The ancient Greeks argued for the existence of a Creator or First Cause. They built on the fundamental idea of Parmenides who early in the fifth century BCE said in simple language that can hardly be improved: "nothing can come from nothing."

This argument was expanded in 1802 by William Paley in some

of the most famous words written on the subject of God and science. I repeat them here because the "watchmaker analogy" is used today to both promote the idea of "Intelligent Design" and by atheist apologists such as Richard Dawkins who wrote the book *The Blind Watchmaker* and *The God Delusion* as a direct critique against the kind of argument that Paley proposed and is still current:

In crossing a heath, suppose I pitched my foot against a stone, and were asked how the stone came to be there; I might possibly answer, that, for anything I knew to the contrary, it had lain there forever: nor would it perhaps be very easy to show the absurdity of this answer. But suppose I had found a watch upon the ground, and it should be inquired how the watch happened to be in that place; I should hardly think of the answer I had before given, that for anything I knew, the watch might have always been there. (...) There must have existed, at some time, and at some place or other, an artificer or artificers, who formed [the watch] for the purpose which we find it actually to answer; who comprehended its construction, and designed its use. (...) Every indication of contrivance, every manifestation of design, which existed in the watch, exists in the works of nature; with the difference, on the side of nature, of being greater or more, and that in a degree which exceeds all computation.

– William Paley, Natural Theology (1802)

The response to Paley's argument in *Natural Theology, or Evidences of the Existence and Attributes of the Deity collected from the Appearances of Nature*, came from Charles Darwin who earlier had been convinced by Paley's evidence. Darwin stated:

The old argument of design in nature, as given by Paley, which formerly seemed to me so conclusive, fails, now that the law of natural selection has been discovered. We can no longer argue that, for instance, the beautiful hinge of a bivalve shell must have been made by an intelligent being, like the hinge of a door by man. There seems to be no more design in the variability of organic beings and in the action of natural selection, than in the course which the wind blows. Everything in nature is the result of fixed laws.

And so the argument has gone for much of the past two hundred years. Machine or God? Naturalists or theists? There is strong orientation toward pure naturalism in the elements of our culture considered the more intellectual, educated and sophisticated including our major media, educational institutions and entertainment industry. We'll explore that orientation more later. Conversely, there is a quite strong anti-naturalism viewpoint— focused on evolution-- seen in the way in which the majority of lives are lived and through the cultural expressions of the church and religion crowd. The antagonism between these two opposite poles in our culture reflects the antagonism and unease that many of us feel inside. It used to be when you listed major cultural institutions or cultural engines as I refer to them, the church stood alongside the media, education and entertainment. But now, a great divide exists with considerable tension between the secular engines and the religious engine.

That divide is played out clearly for most of us in our minds. Most of us live with two different pictures in our head, both claiming absolute truth. We live daily with cognitive dissonance, as the psychologists would say. We believe deeply in two things that cannot simultaneously be true. We are naturalists by education and cultural expectations. We are thoroughgoing theists in our inward, spiritual lives.

We have two minds when it comes to our understanding of the world. That conflict is worked out in ways that may uniquely define our time and history. We cannot as a society really make up our minds if this world is a completely random, meaningless mess or if there is a design, purpose and therefore some kind of meaning behind it all. We don't really know from one day to the next whether our own personal philosophies should be "eat, drink and be merry for tomorrow you die," or whether we should pay more attention to the prodding inside us that Someone is watching who cares what choices we make and what we do with our lives. As a nation we grace our celebrations and national events with prayer and references to God while at the same time declaring that prayer is inappropriate in our educational settings and that ultimately it doesn't matter how we pray or to whom we pray. And we make it both illegal and irrational to mix a consideration of the role of a Creator in scientific work—a phenomenon that would stun and befuddle the scientific giants such as Newton and Galileo on whose shoulders we stand.

This book is a personal exploration of those contrasting viewpoints. It is one person's journey into understanding the truth of our world and what difference that understanding of truth means in one life. We are all on that journey in one form or another. Some take it quite seriously, finding themselves, as I do, hung up between the opposites and being frustrated by the conflict and confusion. For most others I suppose it is more a matter like federal deficits, taxes and the weather—troublesome, perhaps, but not something worth getting steamed up over.

But it does matter to all of us, of that I am convinced. Two days ago I attended a very sad memorial service for a stillborn baby. Carl Sandburg said that a baby was God's opinion that the world should go on. So how do you make sense out of a beautiful life, so perfect and precious in its features, but stilled by an unknown cruelty? How do you answer the grief of two beautiful young parents who so recently were overjoyed with the expectations of a life with their new son? What answer can you give? What explanation?

And how do you even deal with these questions deep inside, questions that bring to the front of your mind the essential questions of life, meaning and purpose?

While I have a point of view as we all do, this is not meant to persuade anyone of my perspective. It is not an apology for theism or atheism. It is not intended as an argument. It is simply part of my lifelong journey in search of truth and reality. In high school, many years ago, I remember having a discussion with friends in which I stated that what mattered most to me was the truth. If someone could prove to me clearly and with compelling evidence that God did not exist, then I would believe it. I would not hold to a faith simply because it provided comfort, peace or other benefits. It had to be true. It was a very conservative, private evangelical high school where this discussion took place.

This journey of truth seeking goes on and will go on to the day I breathe my last. Maybe beyond that. If there is one fond hope I have for those who read it, particularly my children and grandchildren, is that it encourages them to go boldly on in their own journey in search of the truth. And that their prayers may be blessed in the search.

Chapter 2
Isms: Is God There?

Is there a God or is there not? None of us really knows, do we? The most confirmed believer has times of doubts -- that has been recorded over and over. Those who say they never doubt are either saying they never really think about it or are being intellectually dishonest. The same can be said of the avowed atheist.

But even those committed to or inclined to atheism have a difficult time avoiding the instinct to pray in circumstances of great fear or gratitude. In his book *On the Book of Psalms: Exploring the Prayers of Ancient Israel*, Jewish scholar Nahum Sarna recounts a couple of stories of prominent Jewish leaders who had long ago abandoned any personal faith. They each found themselves in difficult circumstances and felt an urge to pray. But, as Sarna retells the experience of one of them, "he needed no effort to suppress the urge because he had not the slightest idea what to say."

While the urge to pray is universal, even among atheists, many of us want to know: Is there a God or isn't there? I am afraid that when it comes to belief in God, or belief in pure mechanism, knowing may be impossible. At least it seems it is quite clearly impossible to "know" right now. From a theistic perspective, if it were possible to know with complete certainty then it would be because God had provided clear and compelling proof. With this kind of proof his existence would be once and forever beyond doubt. "Knowing God" or knowing there is a God would not be a matter of faith and debate, it would only be about acceptance of indisputable truth. He has not done that as evidenced by the many who are very uncertain and the few who are certain he doesn't exist. On the other hand, if science was as conclusive as some seem to believe that everything can be explained and must be explained without resort to God, then only the stubborn and deluded would still believe in a God. Of course, that is what many atheists think about those who are believers. But the truth is a great many very intelligent, very rational, very thoughtful scientists and nonscientists alike believe that God exists and base that belief on the evidence before them—including and increasingly the scientific evidence.

Science, despite how some promote its findings, is not conclusive on the subject one way or the other. But in our culture and our time science is the sacred scripture. It is the body of teaching that is the only widely credible and acceptable source of knowledge. The transition from Christendom to a secular humanist culture inhabited by many believers really is a transition of authority from the Bible and the Church to science. That is why I think it is a little humorous, but mostly sad, to see how many believers continue to attempt to engage those thoroughly wedded to our culture by appealing to the ultimate authority of the Bible or the Church. When appealing to an ultimate authority in a discussion or debate, it is important to appeal to an authority that your audience considers credible. In our culture the Bible and the Church lost that position a long time ago. "Science" is the new Bible, scientists the new priests and preachers, and secular humanism the religious (or cultic as some would say) expression of those teachings.

This is why my own exploration around the question of whether or not God exists is focused primarily on science and not the Bible. Since I was not born in a Hindu culture or an Islamic one, someone appealing to the authority of the Bhagavad-Gita or the Koran would leave me quite unimpressed. Someone thoroughly grounded in our secular and naturalistic culture is similarly unimpressed with appeals to the Bible. However, they and we, since we too are part of that culture, are generally in agreement about appealing to the ultimate authority of science.

Science, however, is pretty confused and confusing on this topic of God or no God. There is plenty of evidence on both sides of the equation when looking at what is "known" right now about our universe or what is generally accepted as the truth by the scientific community. The fact that a thorough understanding of what science teaches us about the universe does not lead inevitably to the conclusion that there is no God will come as a great surprise to some. And that is one of the main points here. I agree with John Polkinghorne, eminent English physicist and cleric, when he says science does not prove that God exists, but neither does it prove that he doesn't. Polkinghorne said, "I don't think we can prove either that God exists or that God doesn't exist – we're in an area of discussion that is too deep for mere proof. I am saying that the existence of the Creator would explain why the world is so profoundly intelligible, and I can't see any other explanation that works half as well."

The scientific evidence against God's existence has been building for some time. The two great milestones of that build up of evidence were the publication of Isaac Newton's observations on the motion of the planets called *Philosophiæ Naturalis Principia Mathematica*, in 1687, and Charles Darwin's publication in 1859 of *On the Origin of the Species.* Both of these books contributed to the perception that explanations for what we observe in our world are best based on natural laws rather than God's specific activities. From a basic understanding of how natural laws result in the motion of the planets through the force of gravity to how the grand diversity of life came into being through natural selection, the "God of the gaps" has been under unrelenting attack.

"God of the gaps" simply refers to the idea that when we can't figure out how something is happening, we assign it to God. For example, when I was very young and heard thunder I did not associate it with lightning. I envisioned what I was hearing as God rearranging the furniture upstairs in his heaven. I suspect it was because one time I heard my mom rearranging furniture upstairs and then when I heard thunder it sounded similar so I quickly imagined it was God doing some interior design work up there. It was a reasonable and somewhat magical explanation to me at the time. When I hear thunder today I still remember that idea even though I learned some time ago that the sound of thunder has somewhat more to do with the explosive effect of lightning on air molecules. And lightning isn't a matter of Zeus or Apollo or some Greek god hurling spears at enemies, it is a massive electrical discharge created by the differences in electrical charges within a cloud or between the cloud and earth.

So, God is not needed for an explanation of lightning or thunder. There is a perfectly reasonable, rational, natural, mechanistic explanation. If the right conditions occur, lightning will strike whether or not God is around to observe it or cause it. And if lightning were to do some damage or take a life, it is not by necessity God's will at work, but merely the blind execution of the laws of nature with some unfortunate soul simply being in the wrong place at the wrong time. Neither is God needed as an explanation for how the planets seem to so reliably orbit each other, nor as an explanation in many scientists' minds as to how life evolved into its many forms.

The successful identification of laws of nature as evidenced by Newton and Darwin led to a great many more such discoveries using similar methods. The trust in these methods, the scientific method, grew along with its success in producing results. And with this success came the increasingly popular idea that God was not needed for any explanation of what was observable in the universe. One of the most famous and earliest expressions of this came through an interchange between Pierre-Simon Marquis de Laplace, one of France's most renowned scientists, and the French emperor Napoleon as recounted by Rouse Ball in 1908:

Laplace went in state to Napoleon to accept a copy of his work, and the following account of the interview is well authenticated, and so characteristic of all the parties concerned that I quote it in full. Someone had told Napoleon that the book contained no mention of the name of God; Napoleon, who was fond of putting embarrassing questions, received it with the remark, 'M. Laplace, they tell me you have written this large book on the system of the universe, and have never even mentioned its Creator.' Laplace, who, though the most supple of politicians, was as stiff as a martyr on every point of his philosophy, drew himself up and answered bluntly, 'Je n'avais pas besoin de cette hypothèse-là.' ("I had no need of that hypothesis.") Napoleon, greatly amused, told this reply to Lagrange, who exclaimed, 'Ah! c'est une belle hypothèse; ça explique beaucoup de choses.' ("Ah, it is a fine hypothesis; it explains many things.")

That exchange supposedly took place in the early 1800s, and while the story may be apocryphal, it is frequently cited because it illustrates a key point. Science was in the early stages of conquering the Christian worldview that assumed a loving God was the Source of all that we see and know. It was also in the early stages of delivering the astounding knowledge and technology upon which our contemporary lives depend. But the debate contained in those two positions lives on. One side says, "I have no need of the hypothesis for the necessity of the existence of a Creator." The other says, "Ah, it is a fine hypothesis; it explains many things."

Noticed I changed Laplace's statement a bit and introduced the idea of "the necessity of God." The reason is because science has not dis-proven the necessity of God. The fact is, with all that we know of the universe, no rational scientist can accurately claim that science proves that God is not needed for the world to be as it is. In his brilliant best seller, *A Brief History of Time*, the famous physicist and cosmologist Stephen Hawking struggles with the question of the necessity of a creator:

"The usual approach of science of constructing a mathematical model cannot answer the questions of why there should be a universe for the model to describe. Why does the universe go to all the bother of existing? Is the unified theory so compelling that it brings about its own existence? Or does it need a creator, and, if so, does he have any other effect on the universe? And who created him?"

Here we have a strange situation. Scientists must proceed with the idea that God cannot be an explanation for what they are studying. To do otherwise would make them theologians and philosophers, not scientists. Can you imagine a researcher pursuing the cause for a particular kind of cancer concluding: "God is the only possible explanation for why this cancer happens." The research game is up. No more grants, no more studies, no more Eureka moments of discovery. No more reason to continue. Science is in one way an intentional process of showing that God is not needed. The laws of nature and natural processes always replace the God of the gaps as an explanation as to how and why things happen as soon as they are discovered.

But, for those areas of study where answers have yet to be found, God remains a necessity. As soon as a rational, verifiable law has been found or a theory proven, God is no longer necessary as an explanation. The moment an Einstein of the future (or one working hard at it today) comes up with a rational, verifiable explanation as to how the universe came into being without the necessity of God, we will have "proof" that God does not *need* to exist. There are theories, of course. Theories like quantum particles popping in and out of existence. The most popular "we don't need God" theory is that of the multiverse. It's the only existing alternative to the fine-tuning argument for design. But all this wildly unproven idea does is push the issue of First Cause an infinite number of universes farther back. There very well may come a time when we can conclude that science shows that it is possible for the world to come into being and exist without a Creator and Sustainer. But, we are not there yet. So, as we will see, today we can quite rationally conclude there is still a big gap that only God can fill.

We mentioned the issue of the fine-tuning of the universe. Scientists now clearly understand that the universe is extremely fine-tuned for life. What does it mean to be fine-tuned for life? It means if any of the various laws, measurements and characteristics of our universe were any different than they are—

even to the most infinitesimal degree—I would not be here trying to explain this and you would not be where you are working these things through your mind. The degree of fine-tuning is greater than can easily be described, but one prominent scientist did a good job of it by equating it to baking a cake. Getting the recipe just right for the cake to taste good is important. But in the recipe of baking the cake of our universe, if just a few grains of sugar were left out of the recipe, the cake would be worthless. That might be surprising enough but it would be true if the cake you were baking were ten times the mass of the sun! That's what fine-tuning of the universe really means. But it is not just one ingredient that had to be just so. It is a number of ingredients with no room for error.

Dr. Hugh Ross lists 93 ingredients that have to be just so. I'll just show the first 20 to give you an idea:

· Strong nuclear force constant
· Weak nuclear force constant
· Gravitational force constant
· Electromagnetic force constant
· Ratio of electromagnetic force constant to gravitational force constant
· Ratio of proton to electron mass
· Ratio of number of protons to number of electrons
· Ratio of proton to electron charge
· Expansion rate of the universe
· Mass density of the universe
· Baryon (proton and neutron) density of the universe
· Space energy or dark energy density of the universe
· Ratio of space energy density to mass density
· Entropy level of the universe
· Velocity of light
· Age of the universe
· Uniformity of radiation
· Homogeneity of the universe
· Average distance between galaxies
· Average distance between galaxy clusters

What makes this even more complex is that many of these are in close interrelationship with each other. That means it's not just the values for each of these items that matters, it is how these values are intertwined with each other.

The fully established fact of fine-tuning in our universe calls for an explanation. With this fine-tuning phenomenon we are saying there is a necessity for God that goes beyond First Cause. First Cause is the classic argument for the existence of God going back to the early Greek philosophers because we all can understand that if there is an action there has to be someone or something that caused that action. But that is true of any action. The fine-tuning is not just any action—it is incredibly precise and necessary action. It even goes beyond saying if there is a machine, there must be a machinist, or if there is a watch there must be a watchmaker. The machine or watch turns out to be precise and complex and incredibly well designed beyond any imagining. God is necessary in the face of such facts, unless one insists that he is not. Then the only other alternative is chance. Coincidence. It just happened that way. We got lucky -- very, very lucky.

John Leslie, an Oxford-trained philosopher from the University of Guelph in Canada in 1989 wrote *Universes*, which carefully detailed many of the dimensions of fine-tuning. He famously used the illustration of the universe being similar in chance to someone facing a firing squad of 50 expert marksmen, and surviving. If you were the survivor, you would have to either conclude that it was a really remarkable coincidence that they all could miss or that somehow you were quite popular with the executioners, and therefore it was intentional.

Since sheer lucky coincidence is the only rational way out of the necessity of God in the face of the finely tuned nature of our world, this is the direction many in science are taking. They see it as their job to do so. If they were to say, "Well, that is it, the game is up, God really does exist after all and that explains everything," they believe, wrongly I think, that that would be the end of science. No, an explanation must be sought and that means finding an answer that does not involve intelligence, intention or will. It had to have just happened by chance. And how could such a universe occur?

Let's let Stephen Hawking, quite certainly not a believer in God, be our guide here. He said, "The whole history of science has been the gradual realization that events do not happen in an arbitrary manner, but that they reflect a certain underlying order, which may or may not be divinely inspired." In other words, a machine requires a machinist. But is a machine, even an extremely complex and finely tuned machine possible without a machinist? Here's Hawking again:

"The remarkable fact is that the values of these numbers seem to have been very finely adjusted to make possible the development of life. For example, if the electric charge of the electron had been only slightly different, stars either would have been unable to burn hydrogen and helium, or else they would not have exploded. Of course, there might be other forms of intelligent life, not dreamed of even by writers of science fiction, that did not require the light of a star like the sun or the heavier chemical elements that are made in stars and are flung back into space when the stars explode. Nevertheless, it seems clear that there are relatively few ranges of values for the numbers that would allow the development of any form of intelligent life. Most sets of values would give rise to universes that, although they might be very beautiful, would contain no one able to wonder at that beauty. One can take this either as evidence of a divine purpose in Creation and the choice of the laws of the science or as support for the strong anthropic principle."

So, there it is. The simple choice elegantly presented by one of the most famous, respected scientists of our day, the man who held Isaac Newton's Lucasian Chair of Mathematics at the University of Cambridge. What is the "strong anthropic principle"?

24

"According to this theory, there are either many different universes or many different regions of a single universe, each with its own initial configuration and, perhaps, with its own set of laws of science. In most of these universes the conditions would not be right for the development of complicated organisms; only in a few universes that are like ours would intelligent beings develop and ask the question: 'Why is the universe the way we see it?' The answer is then simple: If it had been different, we would not be here!"

The "strong anthropic principle" is very academic sounding. But it is the only way out for naturalists who do not wish to or cannot accept the necessity of God. David Lindley rightfully concluded in his book *The End of Physics* that scientist's use of the anthropic principle is in fact their scientifically acceptable way of referring to God:

"The anthropic principle begins to look like a name for the repository in which we set aside all the things that physics cannot yet explain. It is always a last resort...The anthropic principle is used to explain those things for which physics alone, we suspect, cannot provide an answer. It provides the role that less artful scientists in earlier ages ascribed unabashedly to a prime mover, or to God."

So the anthropic principle becomes the scientifically acceptable alternative to the God of the gaps. They must have some other explanation other than God. As Paul Davies points out in *The 5th Miracle*, "However, it is the job of scientists to solve mysteries without recourse to divine intervention." Our current understanding of physics leaves scientists with two very uncomfortable choices: ascribe the impossible coincidences to God or assign them to the most unlikely good fortune anyone could possibly imagine.

The alternatives remain: design or the most remotest chance. The very successful ideas of Darwin regarding natural selection that have been verified by our much more detailed understanding of DNA and the numerous mutations or subtle changes in our genes have been applied to the question of origin of our universe. Darwinists answer the question of how life evolved by demonstrating that random chance is built into the process of communicating genetic information and that the changes that result are sometimes beneficial to the creature. If it improves its chances of survival in a rough world, the modification will be sustained and carried on to future generations.

Chance as a powerful factor in explaining our world came about through Darwin's theories and has been well developed into something called Probability Theory. Things happen by random chance and over time, with enough random changes, it seems almost anything is possible. One of the most often-cited examples of probability theory at work is the idea that if you had enough monkeys in a room typing at typewriters they would at some point in time write a complete Shakespearean sonnet; some say the complete works of Shakespeare. But Israeli scientist Gerald Schroeder has explored this theory to see if there is any truth to it. As quoted by famous former atheist Antony Flew in his book *There Is A God,* here is Schroeder's analysis:

"All the sonnets are the same length. They're by definition fourteen lines long. I picked the one I knew the opening line for, "Shall I compare thee to a summer's day?" I counted the number of letters; there are 488 letters in that sonnet. What's the likelihood of hammering away and getting 488 letters in the exact sequence as in "Shall I compare thee to a summer's day?" What you end up with is 26 multiplied by itself 488 times—or 26 to the 488th power. Or in other words, in base 10, 10 to the 690th.

Now the number of particles in the universe—not grains, of sand, I'm talking about protons, electrons and neutrons—is 10 to the 80th. Ten to the 80th is 1 with 80 zeros after it. Ten to the 690th is 1 with 690 zeros after it. There are not enough particles in the universe to write down the trials; you'd be off by a factor of 10 to the 600th....You will never get a sonnet by chance. The universe would have to be 10 to the 600th times larger. Yet the world thinks the monkeys can do it every time."

If you think that coming up with 488 words in the right sequence is a difficult task for monkeys and the probability theory, try getting the electromagnetic strength just right or the temperature of the cosmological constant. That is far more difficult for chance to accomplish.

The scale by which chance is measured has to do with how big the coincidence is. In other words, if you were trying to unlock a combination lock it is quite possible that with three random spins you could get lucky and happen on the right combination. But what if the lock had twenty different numbers that all had to be right in order? What if it had a thousand? Then the only way random chance would work is if you had a long, long, long time to spin the dial. The bigger the combination, the more spins to happen up on it. And the combination to this lock is huge.

Let me give just one brief example. Stephen Barr in his book *Modern Physics and Ancient Faith* identifies a number of the extreme coincidences included in fine-tuning. Here is just one— the cosmological constant. Don't worry, you don't have to understand the ideas, just look at the magnitude of the measurement:

"In order for life to be possible, then, it appears that the cosmological constant, whether it is positive or negative, must be extremely close to zero—in fact, it must be zero to at least 120 decimal places. This is one of the most precise fine tunings in all of physics."

So the combination lock consists of a lot more than three sequential numbers. For the analogy to work, the combination might have to be millions of numbers long. But in our analogy, for the universe to work in such a way to enable me to be writing this the combination had to be found and the lock opened. Did someone know the combination or was it discovered by chance? Chance would require a great many spins. For chance to work in creating a universe with this kind of fine tuning, there would have to be an awful lot of universes generated out of Big Bangs, each with their own set of randomly developed laws and forces. How many? More than millions, more than trillions. In fact, the only way those who subscribe to the chance idea can deal with it is to suggest that there would have to be an infinite number or close to it.

I was surprised and amused several years ago when I picked up a copy of one of the newsstand magazines that popularizes scientific discoveries. The cover said something to the effect: "Multiple Universes Discovered." Now, this was not the "National Inquirer" or a science fiction magazine. This is a respected scientific magazine aimed at the sophisticated but non-professional science reader. I eagerly picked it up expecting to find evidence somehow of universes beyond our own. Perhaps the science fiction writers were right, that wormholes leading out of black holes led into other universes. No, the "evidence" presented was a simplified version of the fine-tuning principle; in this case focusing on six critical numbers. The article quoted an eminent British astrophysicist as saying that the coincidence of these numbers being just so required the existence of multiple universes. Ergo, proof that they exist.

Let me be clear here. I am not saying at all that multiple universes don't exist. There may be many universes. There may be an infinite number in sizes and scales that we don't understand—easy to consider since I can't get my head around the one we find ourselves in. But what I am saying is that there is no physical evidence, no way we have right now of proving that theory. Yes, there is indication of multiple universes in what is called M-Theory, a part of String Theory that also calls for a universe not with the four dimensions that we are familiar with but with eleven dimensions. I have a hard time getting my mind around that as well. When naturalists believe in something so "out there," so unprovable, so metaphysical, it seems there must be something driving the ready acceptance. To violate the "truth in beauty" idea and ignore Occam's Razor requires a compelling reason. That reason is simply that the alternative is less acceptable. Believing in a completely unproven and likely unprovable idea based on speculation without substantial evidence is far preferable than accepting the possibility of design. This, you might have noticed is no longer science. It is faith. The naturalists, in their eagerness to avoid religion and all its consequences, have moved into the neighborhood. More and more, naturalist scientists are looking like metaphysicians and philosophers. Polkinghorne summarizes this neatly:

"Both of these propositions (many universes or creation) are metascientific in character. The many-universes proposal shares this feature with the proposal of a creation, since science only has direct experience of the single universe open to our observation...Metaphysically, in relation to the Anthropic Principle by itself, there does not appear to be anything to choose between the two explanations proffered. Many worlds and creation seem to be of equal plausibility."

Laplace's children still have no need for the hypothesis of a Creator. But what they have instead is a hypothesis that says chance can do all things given enough time and enough universes. Beyond the Big Bang, mechanists and believers alike wander off into a world of faith in the improbable. Barr concludes this concisely: "It seems that to abolish one unobservable God, it takes an infinite number of unobservable substitutes."

Chapter 3
Quantum World: A Very Strange Place

There is a significant, maybe even huge, gap between what today's science teaches about our world and what most common ordinary non-scientists think science teaches about our world. After reading this, unless you are very scientifically oriented (which I clearly am not) you will likely be quite surprised at how our world is currently understood by the professionals.

There are several reasons for this. One is that much of what has been discovered, particularly about quantum mechanics, is counter intuitive—it is a far cry from what we have come to expect in our world of personal experience. While it has its own internal logic and consistency, It isn't rational or logical in the normal way we have of looking at the world and understanding things. Another related reason is that it is contradictory to the basic understanding we have of our universe—those understandings that are intuitive and do make sense. What is somewhat ironic about this, and we'll explore this thought more later, the very rationality that was discovered in the universe that led our culture to adopt the idea of mechanism can be viewed as undermined by the numerous discoveries of just how strange and irrational our universe really is. This, of course, does not stop naturalists -- nor the rest of us -- from believing in logic and rationality. But quantum mechanics forces us to think about these things in entirely new ways.

This points to the reality that science has become very much like a religion in many people's minds. It is deeply ingrained as part of our culture. With religion invariably you have some form of priesthood. You might call them shamans, or prophets, or witch doctors or pastors. But they form an elite group that separate themselves from the ordinary "believers." Their special powers are related to a higher level of understanding that includes their own private language. They speak of things we know little of. So some of the veil that covers much of today's science is because we on the outside tend to only hear a little of what the scientists are saying to each other, and when we do overhear them talking, they converse in their own special language with jargon, terms and foundational understandings that we are not privy to.

The main reason for walking through this morass of scientific weirdness is to establish the rationality of praying to a God who has room enough to maneuver in the universe to answer prayers. As you will see, believing in such a God is rational given our current understanding of the world. Furthermore, the clearly non-rational beliefs about the reality of our world as explained by scientists today makes those who lay the charge of non-rationality against believers look like the pot calling the kettle black. As you will see, if your mind is open to it, that ideas of what is rational and what is irrational are becoming muddy.

Most of the strangeness we will look at here has to do with what is called Quantum Mechanics. Quantum generally refers to the behavior of elements of our world at the level of atoms and below. The word "quantum" is Latin in origin and is related to "quantity" or how much—how much things weigh, how many there are, how fast something is going—basic ways we have of measuring physical entities. The concept of the atom is not new. The word atom means "uncuttable" and is Greek. It was Greek philosophers who described atoms as the smallest, indivisible particles that made up our world. But we have found that atoms can indeed be divided, and that the forces that hold the atoms together can be so powerful that when we figure out how to divide them in a controlled way, we can unleash tremendous energy. The explosions over Hiroshima and Nagasaki demonstrated to the entire world a fact that scientists had known for some time.

The problem with Quantum Mechanics is that when you start delving into the world of electrons and photons, neutrons and protons, and then go beyond that to quarks, leptons and gluons, things tend to get very strange. We have come to expect, through repeated observations, that things work in a very predictable way in the world as we see and experience it. You throw a rock and it sails through the air until wind resistance and the force of gravity slows it and brings it to earth. You observe the waves on the seashore and you see that there is an almost endless series of peaks and troughs—sometimes calm and peaceful and sometimes massive and frightening. So it is entirely understandable that scientists when delving into the objects that make up atoms and pieces of atoms would expect that those pieces or particles would operate in ways consistent with what we observe. Forces like electromagnetic radiation would flow like waves with peaks and troughs and variable frequency and magnitude. Elements like particles, when moving from one location to another, would behave like a thrown rock or a bullet shot from a rifle.

But when physicists such as Albert Einstein really started looking at the behavior of things at the atomic level, things didn't always work like they were supposed to. Scientists for a long time had tried to understand light. How is it that we see things? What is this thing called light if the entire world is made up of particles and forces? In the early 1800s it was well established that light was a wave—it acted like the waves of the ocean with ups and downs, peaks and troughs and frequency (how far apart the waves were spread out) and amplitude (how big the waves were). In that way it resembled sound and because sound depended on a medium in which to travel, the assumption was that light also traveled in a medium. They called it ether. Then comes Einstein and in 1905, in experiments on the photoelectric effect for which he won the Nobel Prize, he determined that light was made up of particles. Little bits or packets of energy he called photons. Now here was a problem. In 1865 the Scottish physicist and mathematician, James Clerk Maxwell, clearly established that light was a wave and was a form of electromagnetism. But Einstein demonstrated light was a particle. How can something be both like a bullet and water lapping at the seashore?

You and I know there is a great difference between a bullet and a wet wave. But, the brainiacs of the world at the turn of the last century concluded that light was actually a particle **and** a wave. It gets worse—a lot worse. It's not just light that works in this strange way. Everything does. Every little bit of you and me, the desk I'm writing this on, the smelly dog next to me, we are all made up of elements that on the one hand look and act like quivering bits of energy and at the same time like tiny bits of matter that move through time and space like particles. This is called the wave-particle duality and it is as fundamental to our understanding of the world as the force of gravity that keeps the earth moving around the sun and explains why apples fall from trees.

Now, you would think that this mystery of whether matter and energy were really waves or particles could be solved. If we could just get our hands on it and measure it, then we could say with some certainty what the nature of it is without resorting to this kind of mushy-mouthed explanation called the wave-particle duality. Ah, that is a problem, a big problem.

A young German physicist by the name of Werner Heisenberg was looking into this issue of waves and particles. The key was in measurement. But, in 1927 Heisenberg discovered that these bits and pieces of matter, when you got down to the level of photons and electrons could not be measured. There are a couple of ways of measuring physical entities: position and momentum. In other words, we can pretty well figure out where things are at and, if they are moving, how fast they are going. We can describe a car's position at any time—just look at your GPS—and it will also tell you how fast it is going. We know, because our brains and experience tell us that you can measure both position and speed at the same time. Not so with the really small things. When Heisenberg tried to measure these tiny bits of matter he found that he could determine momentum but when he did that he lost all track of its position. Likewise, he could measure its position, but then he had no idea of its momentum. First, Heisenberg thought it had to do with the measuring instruments. But he came up with an elegant mathematical formula for describing this and it became known as the Heisenberg Uncertainty Principle. It is now widely understood that this isn't a problem with measurement instruments, it is a fundamental fact of the elements of our universe at the tiny level—they simply will not be measured in the way in which we intuitively think they ought to be. You can know one thing about them, but you can't know the other and vice versa. It is very much related to the fact that our world is made up of matter and energy that are both waves and particles—and the two can't be the same, but they are.

Hold on, because things are about to get truly weird. Particles are often linked in pairs, such as when they separate from other particles when decaying or when forced apart. These pairs of particles are complementary in that they have a property called "spin" which can be observed. If the spin of one is one direction, the spin of the other is always in the other direction. So this pair is linked, or "entangled" so that what affects one, affects the other. That all makes sense, until scientists discovered that distance made not one bit of difference to this situation. That means if a pair of particles is entangled, their influence or control over each other will stay the same, regardless of how far they get separated. It is sort of like a set of twins who always end each other's sentences. Makes sense if they are in the same room taking part in a single conversation. But imagine if one traveled to the other side of the continent and they continued with this habit. No matter the conversation, they continued to finish each other's sentences at precisely the same time as if they were in the same room.

We all know, don't we, that nothing is faster than the speed of light: 186,000 miles per second. That is very fast. No matter can travel faster than that. Since we have harnessed fiber optics for our computer networks, we can convey information around the globe in milliseconds. It's fast and every known law of science that says you can't go faster—only Star Trek suggests there is "warp speed." So how is it then that two pairs of particles, separated from one end of our universe to the other, can instantly, simultaneously influence or change the other's behavior? I don't know, and the scientists don't know either.

This property was a natural consequence of the Quantum Theory, but Einstein, who seemed to think quantum theory a lot of hogwash, thoroughly disliked it. He called it "spooky action at a distance," and said he'd rather be a cobbler than a physicist if he had to believe things like this. But, he was one of the first to recognize this essential quality of matter based on quantum theory. As Polkinghorne states, "although Einstein was a kind of grandfather of quantum mechanics, he didn't like its later developments and he was always trying to discredit it." In an attempt to prove that there was something fundamentally wrong with quantum mechanics, he and two others, Boris Podolsky and Nathan Rosen, created a thought experiment that demonstrated this "spooky action at a distance" was a necessary consequence of quantum mechanics simply to prove that there was something fundamentally wrong with quantum theory. That's why today this "discovery" is called the EPR paradox for Einstein, Podolsky and Rosen.

While demonstrated mathematically by the three of them, in 1980 physical proof of this strange phenomenon was provided by a clever experiment by some French scientists. There have been many experiments since then that validate this almost unbelievable aspect of quantum mechanics, including those conducted in Geneva in 2008 that set the lower limit of the "speed" of this entanglement at 10,000 times the speed of light. We can only imagine what the upper limit might be.

So now we know that bits and pieces of our world "talk" to each other, or somehow affect each other across the vastness of our universe. But what is our universe made of? Almost everyone would answer that question by saying it is made up of those things we can touch, taste, smell and measure. In more scientific terms it is made up of matter—bits and pieces of real stuff—and of forces, those things like gravity and electromagnetism that determine how the stuff moves around and interacts with each other. In fact, when scientists first started verifying that matter and forces could be used all by themselves to describe just about everything in our world the philosophers grabbed onto this notion and developed a philosophy around this called positivism. It is important to understand this in light of what I am going to tell you shortly about the true nature of our universe, because this idea of positivism is still what largely drives our culture and understanding of reality despite the fact that it has been thoroughly discredited in philosophical circles a long time ago.

Positivism simply states that it ain't real if you can't touch, taste, feel, observe or measure it. Knowledge is limited to our experience—everything else is nonsense. It is called positivism because August Comte promoted the idea that there were three phases of human development: theological, metaphysical and the positive. When the intellectuals began throwing off the ideas of God and metaphysical speculation in the late 1700s and early 1800s, Comte believed we had entered this latest and most advanced phase called the positive. It corresponded exactly to what those enthralled with the new scientific discoveries believed about the world and soon became the dominant philosophy of the Western world and, in many ways, is still the dominant underlying philosophy of our secular culture.

There's a bit of a problem with this view. Scientists now recognize that much of what is real in our universe lies outside the bounds of what we have been able to observe and measure in any traditional sense. Such as these things called dark energy and dark matter. We also have this stuff called anti-particles and anti-matter. If I were to tell you that somewhere in the universe there is an opposite of you, an anti-Diane, an anti-Bob, an anti-Liz, you would think I was talking science fiction. What if I told you that if you ran into your anti-person in another universe that as soon as you connected both of you would be completely annihilated? It would seem even more strange. But such is the truth of our world. We do know that there are electrons and anti-electrons and when the two come in contact they annihilate each other. This happens all the time in nature and is one source of gamma rays. We can create anti-particles and we can even create anti-atoms such as anti-hydrogen. These anti-things obey exactly the same laws of physics as matter and particles but they are opposite. You might think that this means that somewhere there is a mirror universe made up of anti-everything including anti-us but the truth is this anti-world is our world. It makes up an essential element of our world.

Is there a danger of our world being annihilated and ending up as a mass of photons in gamma rays when all the anti-matter collides with matter? Probably not because for some strange reason there appears to be a lot more matter than anti-matter. Since this asymmetry, as it is called, doesn't exactly make sense either, there is the thought that other parts of our universe may have massive amounts of anti-matter. NASA is currently looking into the matter. Think about that if you think I am spouting nonsense. Your tax dollars are at work right now to discover some missing pieces of the universe that most of us didn't have a clue existed, and if they do exist don't make any sense at all. And if NASA does discover this region filled with anti-matter, maybe an anti-Bob or anti-Susan will show up.

While NASA is out looking for anti-matter I'm hoping they also keep a close eye out for dark matter and dark energy. You know about the force of gravity. It's what keeps you in your comfy chair as you read this; it's what forces the thrown ball back to the ground and it's what keeps the planets moving around the sun. You may have also heard that the precise force of gravity is what caused the formation of the stars, galaxies and planets like our own little one we call Earth. Gravity explains a lot, which is why Isaac Newton is so honored and can be rightfully considered the father of naturalism. So if you look out at the big universe and note that the Big Bang explosion is continuing on, but at a specific pace, you can attribute that to gravity—that mysterious force that causes things with mass to be attracted to each other in proportion to their mass. So we can look out at the observable universe, calculate the mass of the stars and planets and galaxies and understand their movements based on the law of gravity. That all makes sense, right?

Here's the problem: based on the laws of gravity there isn't nearly enough visible stuff to account for that movement. So, we either have to throw out everything we know about gravity—which would upset a lot of things. Or we have to account for something we can't see but know must be there because of this very well established law. So we have a division between the visible universe and the invisible universe. Sort of like you can observe the table being set by a real person, but you also see the table being set by itself which you have to attribute to an invisible person. Another analogy, thanks to retired mathematics professor James Bradley, is of a car accelerating. If it is speeding up it is because someone is stepping on the accelerator or it is heading down hill. But our universe, classically understood is on level ground and no one is in the driver's seat. What is the invisible force that is causing the car, our universe, to accelerate?

So, there are visible or known forces and invisible, unknown ones. How much is visible? Only about 4% of our universe. The rest is considered "dark" or invisible. About 22% of that is considered "dark matter" and 74% "dark energy." We know (or believe) it is there because without it our classical understanding of the motion of bodies based on gravity simply won't work. I want to quote directly the Wikipedia explanation for the state of dark matter and energy so you can see for yourself the status of this in terms of contemporary scientific knowledge:

"As important as dark matter is believed to be in the universe, direct evidence of its existence and a concrete understanding of its nature have remained elusive. Though the theory of dark matter remains the most widely accepted theory to explain the anomalies in observed galactic rotation, some alternative theories such as MOND and TeVeS have been proposed. None of these alternatives, however, have garnered widespread support in the scientific community."

I just want to stop here for a moment and point out the challenge that this represents to those who cling to a fully naturalistic view of reality. Dark matter and dark energy are invisible, unobservable and fully accepted as a reality because our understanding of the universe won't work without them. They are mathematically required, therefore we know they must exist. Is it irrational to believe in such unverified entities? Why do some, with a great sense of intellectual superiority, cling to the idea that anyone who believes in something unverified (in the sense of observation and measurement in scientific terms) is a religious nutcase? All the while believing in ideas, entities and constructs that are both strange and unproven? That, I am convinced, is one clear proof of the dissonance we face in our culture as we try to come to grips with the two world views, our two minds.

Note that the necessity of dark matter and energy, plus the inexplicable behavior of particles at the quantum level are all well accepted because they have been proven mathematically. We have come to so trust in the reliability of this way of structuring our understanding of the universe that in many ways the old way of learning about reality has been reversed. It used to be that we would carefully observe something, then create a theory based on our observations. That theory could then be tested by experiment or observation. If we saw it repeated reliably enough, we may conclude that what we were observing described a fundamental law or principle. But now quite often discoveries are made with mathematics first. Physicists look at a puzzle and try to work out the answer mathematically. If an elegant or "beautiful" solution is created, that is taken as evidence of the reality behind the math. Then experiments are conducted to see if the math is indeed correct. Those experiments usually confirm the reality of the math and so we have come to place high confidence in this math-first method. One of the most powerful, literally powerful, examples of this was Einstein's exceedingly simple and elegant formula: $e=mc^2$. Energy equals mass times the speed of light squared. That little formula proved to have accurately predicted the power that was unleashed a number of years later in the detonation of the world's first atomic bomb on July 16, 1945 near White Sands, New Mexico. Barely three weeks later 120,000 Japanese were killed with the world's first nuclear weapons. Such is the predictive power of mathematics when it is beautiful—the formula, that is, not the devastating results.

However, things are not always what they seem with mathematics only. Even before the atomic was dropped, an Austrian mathematician and philosopher by the name of Kurt Gödel shocked the naturalistic world. He proved, using math, of course, that math had its limits. That there were inherent limits to what mathematics could say about the reality of our world. Here's what Stephen Hawking says about Gödel's "incompleteness theorem" in his book *The Universe in a Nutshell*:

"In 1931 the mathematician Kurt Gödel proved his famous incompleteness theorem about the nature of mathematics. The theorem states that within the formal system of axioms, such as present day mathematics, questions always persist that can neither be proved nor disproved on the basis of the axioms that define the system. In other words, Gödel showed that there are problems that cannot be solved by any set of rules or procedures.

Gödel's theorem set fundamental limits on mathematics. It came as a great shock to the scientific community, since it overthrew the widespread belief that mathematics was a coherent and complete system based on a single logical foundation. Gödel's theorem, Heisenberg's uncertainty principle, and the practical impossibility of following the evolution of even a deterministic system that becomes chaotic, form a core set of limitations to scientific knowledge that only came to be appreciated during the twentieth century."

Brian Cox and Jeff Forshaw, two of the most respected popularizers of science today make clear the limits of scientific understanding in the preface to their book *Why Does E=MC²: (And Why Should We Care?*: "In science there are no universal truths, just views of the world that have yet to be shown to be false." This is quite clearly overstating the case. After all, who doubts the law of gravity--even if in its details it is still being refined. Still, some level of humility is called for when dealing with scientific "facts." One could wish that those evangelists for atheism on the basis of scientific certainty would approach these questions of truth and reality with a little more modesty and a little less arrogance.

One of the truly strange things that quantum physicists have apparently discovered about our natural world is the role of conscious observation in bringing the world into existence. This topic continues to cause plenty of discussion, discomfort and avoidance in the science community. We will explore what this means further in a later chapter but let us simply introduce this, another mystery, in the words of physicists Bruce Rosenblum and Fred Kuttner who wrote *Quantum Enigma: Physics Encounters Consciousness*:

"The experimental results (of quantum mechanics) we report and our explanation of them with quantum theory are completely undisputed. It is the **mystery** these results imply beyond physics that is hotly disputed [their emphasis]. For many physicists, this mystery, the quantum enigma, is best not talked about. It displays physics' encounter with consciousness. It's the skeleton in our closet."

These physicists' straightforward treatment of the facts of today's physics leads them to something we find a little unusual in the sciences—the realization that some things may be beyond the scientific approach to understanding. I mentioned humility, which accurately describes the somewhat unusual take these respected physicists have on a very important issue in science today:

"Though the quantum enigma has confronted physics for eight decades, it remains unresolved. It may well be that the particular expertise and talents of physicists do not uniquely qualify us for its comprehension. We physicists might therefore approach the problem with modesty—though we find that hard."

It is not my intention here to try to summarize in a few paragraphs the current state of understanding of our physical world. We've just casually mentioned a few of the very strange things that scientists are learning about our world:

- matter and energy are interchangeable
- most of the world is "dark and invisible"
- for every particle there is an anti-particle that can annihilate it
- matter "communicates" instantaneously across impossible distances
- everything exists in two states simultaneously—waves and particles
- the "measurement problem" or "quantum enigma" suggests reality depends in some way on conscious observation

This is just the beginning of what science teaches us today about our world.

There are two things I would like you to think about as you ponder these things. First, is the huge disparity between how the scientists understand our world and how the rest of us understand it based on what we are led to believe by those who drive our cultural engines. Second, is the underlying weirdness and non-intuitiveness of our current understanding of the world. This understanding is an important beginning point to talk about who God might be and how we can be rationally praying to him.

Chapter 4
Butterflies, Golf and Miracles

I was playing golf with a good friend when he commented on our persistent lack of improvement in the game. "Chaos theory," I replied. Accustomed to such smart aleck comments from me, he showed little interest in this response but I persisted anyway. "Chaos theory states that complex systems are extremely sensitive to initial conditions so that the slightest variations in those conditions can result in massive changes in the outcomes." He shook his head and hit a drive that landed very nicely on the fairway in perfect position for his approach shot.

But I went on. "You know those machines used for testing clubs and golf ball designs, the ones that hit the ball exactly the same way every time? Even in those cases the ball doesn't always land in the same spot. Depends on atmospheric conditions, anomalies in ball materials or club materials, and many other things. So even if I could do much better at controlling all the mechanics of my swing, which I clearly can't, it would still be a frustrating game because of all the other factors that determine where my ball actually lands." By this time he was completely ignoring me just as I was going to get into the story of the butterfly effect.

The butterfly effect states that a complex system like weather is so sensitive to initial conditions that a butterfly flapping its wings in China (or Brazil--I've heard different versions) can affect the weather in Texas (or the US). This idea was quite a change from the long held belief about our world called determinism. The French scientist who we met earlier, Marquis Laplace, the one who told Napoleon he had no need for the hypothesis of God, believed that since the world was operated by fixed mathematical laws as identified by Newton, once you knew all those laws you would know everything that happened.

Everything was set by those laws; all things were determined.

Even though Laplace is strongly identified with this idea of strict determinism, John Barrow in *New Theories of Everything* points out that R. J. Boscovich wrote in 1758:

"Now if the law of forces were known, and the position, velocity and direction of all the points at any given instant, it would be possible for a mind of this type to foresee all the necessary subsequent motions and states, and to predict all the phenomena that necessarily followed from them."

It may sound as if Boscovich was suggesting this is a way to understand God's omniscience, or ability to know everything all at once. If one were capable of knowing all the laws of motion and forces and knew where everything was at a particular point in time, one could know what affect those laws would have on all things and therefore know the future as well as the present. Time would literally have no meaning with this kind of knowledge because what happened in the past, future, and present would all be clear based on the law of forces.

Barrow writes:

"In a completely deterministic world, all the information about its structure is implicit in the initial conditions. The existence of time is a mystery. There is no use for it...the deterministic straightjacket makes time appear superfluous. Everything that is ever going to happen is explicit in the starting state."

But of course, Boscovich and particularly Laplace were not suggesting that such knowledge was held in the domain of God alone, but would be accessible to finite minds providing we were able to gain enough knowledge about the law of forces and the position of things. Such thinking was understandable in the atmosphere following Isaac Newton's remarkable accomplishment in using mathematics to describe the motion of the planets and to connect this motion with our everyday experience of things falling to earth. Such mathematical beauty and precision, when applied to all forces and all matter, would reveal all things. The planets don't move around the sun because, as Aristotle suggested, it was their inherent tendency to do so. They move because the masses of the sun and the planets drew them to each other and they did not crash because of the balancing force of the law of motion known as inertia. They orbited because they were built to orbit as a clock's pendulum is built to swing based on the pull of the weight. Neither the pendulum nor the planets needed God to keep saying "swing" or "orbit" but instead these objects had no option to do as they were doing because the laws were inexorable—they could not be broken.

Determinism is still an essential element of scientific inquiry, particularly in physics but also in other sciences. The search for how our universe got started has largely been the search for the initial conditions believing that knowledge of those conditions will explain all the various phenomena we observe today. As Barrow mentions, the rigid determinism of Leibniz and Laplace "underpins the majority of the day-to-day concerns of physical scientists whose work is not directly affected by the ambiguities of quantum mechanics."

If our world as defined by our cultural engines is thoroughly mechanistic and naturalistic, as I have suggested, then it is easy to see the continuing role of determinism in our thinking. The ideological opponent to determinism is free will and therefore, by the very use of the words, this conflict has served as a flashpoint between the competing religions of secular naturalism and theism. If the universe is a vast machine and we leave aside for a moment how and why such a machine came into existence, and the machine is highly reliable and predictable, then it makes sense to assume the more we know about how the machine works the more we will be able to predict the results. To find out how the machine works, we can look at the results we see, such as in the observable universe, and create theories and mathematical proofs that identify the laws and required initial conditions. This understanding is in one respect what the entire scientific enterprise is about. If we take away the assumptions of reliability, of completely predictable laws with predictable results, then you have to wonder why we would search for the answers at all. If gravity turned out to be a random sort of thing, sometimes it worked, sometimes it didn't and we could detect no pattern, no rhyme or reason to its variability, we would rather quickly tire of the game and go on to try and find answers to more promising questions. Reliability is an essential element of our science and what makes the "laws" laws. They must be obeyed.

But taken to its logical conclusion, determinism does away with free will and certainly does away with the need for God. Maybe God was needed at the beginning to get the whole machine built and kick-started, but once that was done, the machine runs reliably and unalterably leaving no room for God to exercise his will and certainly no need for it. It is easy to see why in the intellectual ferment of the Enlightenment when these ideas of mechanism were developing, along with the ideas of liberty and the will of the people, so many of the intellectuals of that day were Deists. There may have been the Watchmaker of Paley's description, but once the watch was made and wound up it was very much on its own.

There, is of course, considerable underlying truth to the idea of the universe as a machine and therefore the concept of determinism. Because it is a foundational principle of science, its fundamental tenets cannot and will not be abandoned. Even though the props have been thoroughly kicked out from under the idea of determinism, we continue our search for underlying laws that will answer the questions as to why things happen as they do. We certainly believe that our genes, which we inherited from our parents, have a lot to do with the kind of people we are. We also know and understand that the chemical processes in our brains, themselves a matter of atoms and molecules interacting with each other, are based ultimately on laws that control these interactions. What we have a much harder time with accepting is the logical consequences of rigid determinism which states that the fact that I am now typing these exact words while flying on an airliner at 35,000 feet on the way to a speaking engagement in Topeka, Kansas, was all precisely determined at the instant of the Big Bang. Strict determinism says that as much as I may be fooled into thinking I am free to write what I want, type what I want, think what I want, it is all an illusion because my thoughts are nothing more than electrical synapses controlled by chemicals and atoms and quarks and gluons whose exact behavior at this very moment was a direct and fixed consequence of all the laws that came into existence with our universe 13.7 billion years ago.

There were two primary ideas or understandings of our world that have greatly diminished the confidence in determinism. One is quantum mechanics, most specifically Heisenberg's Uncertainty Principle; the other is chaos theory. The Uncertainty Principle, a very strange idea but clearly supported by the work of countless physicists since it was developed in 1927 by Walter Heisenberg says, in effect, that we can't know what we think we ought to know about particles. Specifically, we can't know simultaneously the momentum of a particle and its location. Chaos theory, as stated earlier in this chapter, says that in a complex system any small change can introduce huge changes that ultimately become unpredictable.

For some reason billiard balls are used a lot in science writing as an analogy for the challenges of chaos theory and also to describe how particles behave. Maybe a lot of physicists like playing pool, or snooker if they are English. Applied to The Uncertainty Principle, we find we might be able to identify where a billiard ball is on a table but if we know that we can't know its speed. Billiard balls in the world of particles are always moving, but if we can measure a ball's speed, doing so will make us lose track of exactly where it is. It could be anywhere at that point. It is just physically impossible to know both. And since momentum or movement and location can make a lot of difference, it means that there is a certain randomness and unpredictability about these particles like photons and electrons and protons.

Using the billiard ball analogy in chaos theory, a strict determinist would say that if you know the initial conditions, such as speed of the hit of the pool cue plus the other conditions, such as how much friction was in the felt on the table, you would be able to precisely determine where all those balls would go after they were struck. But chaos theory says, no you can't. Because the problem is that all those interactions of the balls hitting each other and then bouncing off and hitting others are so complex that the smallest, infinitesimal variation throw it off and mess up the prediction of where the balls would go. In reality, we can measure billiard ball momentum and position very accurately. Professor Bradley pointed out the uncertainty in the product is on the order of 10^{-38} -- extremely small! But, as small as that may be, it is still suggests indeterminacy.

There are really two problems with determinism. One is that systems at the macro-level can be so unutterably complex and so hypersensitive to any change that determining what will happen is just simply impossible. At the micro-level, quantum mechanics says you absolutely can't know some things that would be essential to know even if you had the capability of capturing it all to predict what would happen.

Barrow argues that these two sources of indeterminacy may intersect. Referring to Henry Poincare who was one of the first to point out in the late 1800s that our knowledge would be too inexact for determinism to really work, Barrow writes:

"What we now know what Poincare did not is that quantum aspects of reality forbid the acquisition of such error-free knowledge of the initial conditions in principle, not merely in practice. Nor are these quantum restrictions far removed from experience. If we were to strike a snooker ball as accurately as the quantum uncertainty of Nature permits, then it would take merely a dozen collisions with the sides of the table and other balls for this uncertainty to have amplified to encompass the extent of the entire snooker table. Laws of motion would henceforth tell us nothing about the individual trajectory of the ball."

Whether you agree that quantum uncertainty and chaos theory are linked or not, prediction in the sense of strict determinism becomes impossible. What happens in complex systems is left to chance or randomness. We cannot know the future no matter how utterly complete our knowledge of initial conditions is because the initial conditions themselves will always have an element of randomness.

What that means is that there certainly appears to be room for choice. In fact, on April 13, 2009 John Conway of Princeton University in a lecture at Princeton that has been widely viewed on the Internet, provided a proof that particles themselves have free will. This has to do with the EPR paradox introduced by Einstein Podolsky and Rosen and discussed in an earlier chapter. The "spooky action at a distance" in which the behavior of one of a paired twin of particles is affected, it simultaneously affects the behavior of its twin no matter how many light years they may be apart.

If it turns out that strict determinism doesn't work and prediction of the future is based on extensive knowledge of initial conditions, what does this say about God? Can God know the future if it is random? More importantly, can God exercise his will given the "slop" in the deterministic system that not only provides for randomness and uncertainty but positively demands it? Conway says that since we have free will, the particles that make us have free will and that is indeed why we have free will. But does this mean then that God has free will in the universe as well?

It brings us to a very central question about prayer. What is the point of prayer if God does not, cannot or will not act? Certainly there are prayers of thanksgiving in which nothing is sought but the worshiper only wishes to express his or her appreciation for the grace visible in their experience. And there are prayers of alignment to help us align our thinking and actions with God's purposes. I agree with Polkinghorne in that these prayers should be the focus of how we pray. However, everyone who prays, and as you know I mean by that everyone, prays that God will take some action. We believe when we pray that somehow we can align his will and purpose with our own. There are prayers for finding an empty parking space at the mall, or finding a special pair of tennis shoes on sale. There are desperate prayers to save the life or restore the health of a loved one. There are prayers for assistance to get us out of a tough spot; prayers for understanding and enlightenment, for patience, for courage and strength. Do any of these mean anything?

Miracles have long been a major stumbling block for those who take science seriously, including, of course, believers. In fact, it is one of the top three reasons identified as why thoughtful people have problems with the claims of Christianity (the others being the presence of evil and the divinity of and/or the exclusive claims of salvation through Jesus). When you understand the world as Newton described it and as Leibniz and Laplace extrapolated, there is no room for miracles. The laws are fixed, unbreakable. Water does not turn into wine at a spoken word, dead people do not come to life again, and the sun does not stop in the sky to allow a difficult battle to come to victorious conclusion. Actually, that last one has caused me a lot of trouble, too. It is one thing to think of the sun stopping in the sky when you see the earth as the center of the universe and the sun, moon and stars ringing around it. Sure, why not stop the circling around for just a bit? But when you understand that it is the earth circling around the sun and spinning on its axis that creates a day and night, how does that work? For the sun to stop, the earth would have to stop spinning. Inertia says we'd all fly off in one direction. Hard to picture how that particular miracle about Joshua fighting against the Canaanites could have worked.

It seems rational to me that the laws of nature are fixed. That this fixed nature gives our world its predictability, and science its power. As Professor Bradley explains, the laws of nature are God's covenant with his creation. To break them would be to break this very important agreement. Which leaves the dilemma of prayer: if God does not break the laws of nature how can he answer prayer? And if he answers prayer, does it mean he is violating the very laws of nature he established to make our universe possible?

This is a core question here: is an answer to prayer a miracle? Is praying for something asking God to violate that precious covenant on your behalf? Does praying for a beautiful day for your outdoor wedding involve asking God to rearrange the laws of the universe on your behalf? It certainly does in a deterministic universe, one in which all the initial conditions have precisely determined all outcomes. Whether or not it pours on Saturday for the wedding was fixed at the moment of the Big Bang—all that was left for the necessary consequences to fully unfold. Of course, the believer could say, but yes, God could have known that I would pray for sunshine and he could have built that into the fabric of the universe. Yes, that might work. But such extraordinary planning turns out not to be necessary when the idea of strict determinism is displaced. It might be random or chance that the butterfly in China flapped its wings in such a way to influence the high pressure system coming in from the Canadian prairies so that Saturday turns out to be beautiful. But since that butterfly flapping its wings, or the duck rising from a pond on those prairies could so impact the weather, and since whether or not the wing flappings occur can be based on the random direction or movement of an electron it is just as possible that God could exercise his free will and help that little electron along. Nothing in that violates any laws of nature. There is no way of detecting or knowing whether the change in spin, slight reduction in energy, or random decay of an atom was purposeless or purposeful. We can believe, but we cannot know. We cannot in these circumstances deduce chance from purpose.

Do you believe in coincidence or do you think that all things have a purpose? Or, does it matter the degree of coincidence before it becomes plain to you that what happened seemed to have been predestined? Most of us would think that if you flip a coin a thousand times and you get a 50/50 split between heads and tails, the results are demonstrably random. If you get a 90/10 split for heads, you either have to attribute that to quite remarkable circumstance or suspect that the coin might be weighted.

It is scientifically impossible to tell why a particular particle is at one location and not at another, or traveling at such speed and not another. But does that mean because it does not matter to science that its location is random, mere chance, only coincidence? It does if your presupposition is that there is no motive, no will, no power with intention to decide where that particle will be at any particular moment. But, if your presupposition is that there is such a Being who has the knowledge and power to affect such minute actions, and further has the will out of love, then such things go beyond mere chance.

What this means is that you and I have several completely coherent options when it comes to what happens in our world. We are free to believe in the incredible power of randomness in determining what happens in this world. We are also free to believe that nothing really happens by chance or we can believe that some things happen by chance and some things, that look completely random, are influenced or controlled. One of these choices is not more rational than another from a scientific standpoint because you can't determine whether something is random or intended.

You certainly can't by looking at an individual event. But maybe using the methods of statistical mechanics that have come to be so important in almost all the sciences, you can help decide if things are truly random or caused by the will of God. Statistical studies became important in the sciences in part because of the emerging role of randomness or chance. Statistical analysis was needed to tell a result, such as throwing a handful of sand on a

52

piece of paper, was truly random or if the distribution of the grains was influenced by some other factor. In cosmology it was important when looking at the distribution of matter in the universe which indicated that the unevenness of the distribution was not due to random scattering of matter after the Big Bang explosion. Some force was at work determining the distribution and that force is now generally accepted as massive inflation shortly after the birth of the universe.

But if statistics, or drawing conclusions from observing a collection of results or numbers, can be used to determine if the results are purely random or influenced by some other action, cannot this same method be used to determine the effectiveness of prayer? Indeed, some studies have been done following numerous reports about the effectiveness of faith and prayer in the recovering of seriously ill patients to determine if prayer itself has any impact on recovery. Like most scientific studies, these seem to have mixed results. This does not keep you or I from evaluating the results of our prayers to see if we sense a pattern of response that would indicate more than random chance is at work when we pray. Again, it seems to come down to faith and our presuppositions.

What I have tried to point out here is that it is very possible, given our understanding of science and the withdrawal from strict determinism, that we are free to act in this world. Furthermore, God is also free to act and he can do so without breaking the laws of nature. The old idea of God's actions or intervention in the course of nature being miraculous must change. If this is true, we can pray for healing, for weather, even for parking spaces at the mall without thinking that we are asking for a temporary suspension of the reliable laws of the universe on our behalf. Given the uncertainty principle and chaos theory, there is more than enough "slop" in the system that is our universe to allow purposeful action to take place without violating any of the highly reliable laws that science and our existence depends on. But, does that hold true for miracles as well?

Polkinghorne draws some very useful distinctions between the kind of actions that God is free to take in the world based on this "slop," and miracles. In this he argues against C. S. Lewis' well-known defense of miracles in his book by that title. Lewis wrote in a time when quantum mechanics was a little known and even less understood discussion among the leading physicists and had not reached any level of popular awareness. That means it was still very much a time of acceptance of strict determinism as an almost universal axiom of science and that meant that any intervention of God in the activities of the universe could be considered a violation of the laws of nature. Lewis defended the idea of Providence based simply on the rather reasonable approach, which most of us I think were taught to accept, that if God is powerful enough to bring the universe and all its laws into existence he certainly is not constrained in temporarily breaking those laws. Now it appears that in many cases that we might before have considered miraculous, it is perfectly reasonable to see God's hand behind a result without a single law having been broken. The sunshine for that wedding may have indeed been an answer to prayer fully consistent with the strict laws of science rather than a miraculous intervention in those laws. In this understanding there is a big difference between everyday providence and miracles.

Which is not to say that God cannot, or will not or has not broken any of these laws for his purposes. Certainly, if the story of Joshua's extended battle is true and the sun really stood still in the sky then it was necessary either for the earth to have come to a grinding halt in its movements or for mass hysteria on the part of the observers to have seen it as if it did happen. The situation of the resurrection of Jesus stands in a little different position than the lengthy battle, the miracles of feeding the five thousand, changing water to wine and even the virgin birth. One might argue that some of these miracles might even be possible with only minor violations of the laws of nature. But as for the resurrection, there is nothing minor about that. Certainly not minor in the inviolate laws of death of living beings and all that means, but also not minor in the role that that miracle plays in the belief system of any orthodox Christian. Take the resurrection away, and as Paul pointed out, there is no content left in the religion worth keeping. It is foundational to the faith. At the same time, the complete, final and everlasting reversal of the process of death that is presented in the resurrection is an unprecedented violation of the laws of nature. The earth standing still pales in comparison with the idea that carbon-based life with all its complex processes moving inexorably to recycling, can be transformed into a form of life capable of interacting with humans, but operating in completely and totally new ways with apparently an entirely new set of rules.

This is not God influencing the decay rates of atoms, moving an electron in its orbit just a little into one of many different possible positions or speeds—all of which would be perfectly permitted by known laws. This is an overt, loud and complete overturning of some of the most basic understandings we have of life and nature. Here we cannot turn to minor tweaking and offer it as one alternative in an infinite variety of acceptable choices—this means a different world has broken into this one. A world with laws governing it quite different from our world of everyday existence. This is closer to the multi-verse in impact. This is wormhole science if it was science and not theology. This is a miracle in every sense of the word. Nothing short of a Mind with the capability of creating the rules in the first place and operating completely outside of the created universe would have the capability of so thoroughly breaking and rewriting the rules.

I offered the idea earlier that rational people could choose pure chance or random activity to explain results, or we could choose God's purpose behind all actions, or we could choose a mix. There is a problem with this and it gets to the very heart of one of the most significant theological questions throughout the history not just of Christianity, but of theism. Is God in control or not? Theologically, both the issues of the sovereignty of God and theodicy, or the problem of God's role in the evil we see and experience, are involved. Because if God is behind all those random choices, if they in effect are used to exercise his will and purposes in the world, then must he not also bear responsibility for the disastrous results? Critics of religion have focused on some of the inherent cruelties of nature to question God's role in creation, let alone his love or beneficence. Most recently, fundamentalist atheist Richard Dawkins points to a parasite that invades the body of another animal and kills it in order to follow its evolutionary requirements. If God has freedom in the development of evolutionary processes through the activity at the particle stage, could he not have devised a more decent way for such an animal to exist, or better, yet, made sure that it never came into existence? What after all, is the point of slugs and mosquitoes? More seriously, if we can pray and believe that Aunt Shirley can be cured of her cancer through our fervent prayers because God is behind all these things, how can we avoid the question that God is responsible for her cancer in the first place? If he can arrange the chemical processes to overcome the devastating cell growth of the cancer, could he not also have prevented it from starting, not just in her case, but in every ones?

This is a troubling question for anyone who wishes as I do to believe that ultimately there is purpose and meaning beyond the randomness and chance of our world. But in confronting this perplexing question I find an answer in the way in which Jesus taught his disciples to pray. He taught them to appeal to the Father and to ask that his will be done on earth as it is in heaven. There is an implication in this prayer that is important to our discussion. We live on earth and that means the Father's will is not always done here. If it were, why would Jesus have taught us to pray for his will to be done? He also states that there is a place or a world or a realm called heaven and heaven is where God's will is done perfectly. The contrast is quietly but powerfully drawn. Earth is where God's will is not always done, heaven is where it is always done. But, we can pray, presumably with effect, that earth may come to resemble heaven more in relation to its obedience to God's will.

If will is exercised at the particle level, if all agency or purpose or intention starts at this most foundational level of existence, then it means that one of several things occurs there. We can rationally and logically believe the interactions of particles are completely random; we can believe they are controlled by a Mind and Purpose; we can believe they are strictly determined by the laws of nature; or we can believe in some combination of these agents. We know now that there is no strict determinism found at the particle level based on the Uncertainty Principle, and when we get beyond the particle level into complex systems, the uncertainties only multiply into the chaos theory. Scientists consider everything that happens not determined by fixed laws to be purely random. Theists must believe then that either all (or some) are controlled by Mind/Purpose (God) or by random activity, or -- and there is another alternative -- by a Mind/Purpose that is anti-God. This raises the question of evil and more specifically the personification of evil—a topic that is almost taboo in serious discussions about science and faith.

I've noticed that contemporary Christian writers on these topics, including the likes of Polkinghorne and N.T Wright, sound a little tentative, even squeamish, when bringing up this subject of evil and intentional or personal actions of an Evil One. Understandable. It doesn't fit at all into our contemporary picture of how the world works. The medieval images of a red-suited, forked tail devil luring people into the flaming pit of hell has become an embarrassment for much of the thinking Christian world today. But, there are three realities that we have to deal with when bringing this topic up: 1) personifying evil has been a human intuition that runs as deep as the concept of God; 2) it is part of the biblical story from the very beginning; and 3), Jesus and the gospel writers did not shy away from it but focused significant attention on the personal face of evil.

Does this mean that Satan, or Lucifer, or a fallen angel has been given access to the same particle processes and impact on chaos as we have suggested God may be able to control? On the one hand, this makes much more sense than saying cancer or a pathological mind that results in mass murder requires a violation of the laws of nature in order for us to see intentional evil at work in it. We don't really want the devil to have enough power to interfere with the fixed laws of the universe. On the other hand, does messing with the wavefunction of an electron and so influencing a body's resistance to a fatal disease imply that the Evil One has God-like powers? Consider the uncomfortable story of Job. It appears a clear-cut case where Satan requested and received powers from God to kill Job's children, take away his wealth and afflict his body with horrible disease. If we accept the idea that agency operates at the level of particles and the Uncertainty Principle, then we must say that Satan has access to influencing life, death and experience at this level as well. That thought must cause a chill for those who believe such a thing might be possible. I cannot say the words of the Lord's Prayer, "and deliver us from the Evil One," in quite the same way after considering this possibility.

Chapter 5
Evolution: Whale Hands and a World that Makes Itself

In the late 1800s there were two competing forces pulling at the hearts and minds of all thinking men and women like starving men fighting over a piece of meat. Then a sharp sword came down and split that carcass and the world in two with both sides tumbling far apart from each other. Our culture has been sharply divided into two antagonistic and warring camps ever since. That sharp two-edged sword was the work of a quiet, gentle and heartbroken man who had once studied to become a pastor. Instead, he became a naturalist, took a job on a ship exploring the world and his keen observations of the animals he observed led him to write *The Origin of the Species*. Charles Darwin became the patron saint of those who believe that belief in God is an evil and a delusion that must be fought and who champion a naturalistic worldview with its religion of secularism. For the other side, theists who accepted the biblical story of creation as literal truth, he became the personification of all that was wrong, evil and destructive with the scientific replacement for the Christian view of life.

Evolution, the theory or understanding of the development of life from lower forms to higher forms, remains the primary battlefield in the ongoing clash between the competing world views of mechanistic secularism and theistic belief. What understanding is correct? What is true?

Did God create man with his hands by a river as so beautifully described in the poem by African-American poet James Weldon Johnson:

Up from the bed of the river
God scooped the clay;

And by the bank of the river
He kneeled him down;
And there the great God Almighty
Who lit the sun and fixed it in the sky,
Who flung the stars to the most far corner of the night,
Who rounded the earth in the middle of his hand;
This great God,
Like a mammy bending over her baby,
Kneeled down in the dust
Toiling over a lump of clay
Till he shaped it in is his own image;

Then into it he blew the breath of life,
And man became a living soul.
Amen. Amen.

What magnificent imagery; so intimate, loving, and earthy. The great power of all creation down on his knees, working the dirt and mud of his own creation into the crowning work of all the universe. Then giving this lifeless dust not just the life to live and breathe and breed, but to think, and ponder, and wonder and worship.

Or is it true that the quarks and leptons scattered about by the Big Bang clumped together into atoms pulled together by nuclear forces and the huge dust clouds of those atoms in turn clumped together into massive balls by the force of gravity with such density that they ignited into massive stars which when their energy was consumed collapsed into themselves with giant explosions that created the heavier elements of carbon? And these bits of burnt stardust coalesced with other elements, collecting together in balls of matter called planets? And on one particular planet called earth the conditions of atmosphere and matter were just so, so that something mysterious happened and the matter organized itself in such a way to be able to take in nutrients and to replicate itself and also all of its own to change itself in minute ways? And those minute, occasional, random changes allowed this very simple life to become increasingly well adapted to the environment it found itself in and in this way improved its ability to sustain itself and pass on its capabilities to future generations. Until finally, over millions of years, those changes have resulted in a human being once again sitting on an airplane at 35,000 feet flying to Houston and trying to decide of the two competing ideas about truth which is more likely?

Scientists, particularly those in the esoteric world of elementary particle physics, have a strong tendency toward any theory and any mathematical solution which is beautiful. As David Lindley states "scientists have come to believe that a simple and elegant theory is a better explanation—closer to the truth—than a complex and arbitrary one." If that is the case and I was a scientist, which clearly I am not, there is little doubt in my mind which of the two theories described above is more aesthetically attractive. There is also little doubt as to which is simpler and therefore also passes the test of Occam's Razor. The theory of evolution not only violates the simplicity and beauty test (always subjective, but generally agreed), it also flies in the face of one of the most fundamental laws of classical physics, the second law of thermodynamics. This one says quite simply that in our observable universe, the movement of things is always from order to disorder. In the interaction of material, such as the stuff in my closet, it will not of its own get more orderly but more disorderly. Even if you take out of the picture my personal interaction with that stuff which inevitably produces disorder, the nature of the material is such that it will decay and rot and disintegrate so that what is left over time is much less orderly than what was in there when I last left it. To say that the materials of the world have the capability all of their own using laws of nature to go from the disorder of an exploding star into the massively complex order that is life itself and the brain in particular is, if true, the most astounding violation of this inviolate law that can be imagined. To accept such nonsense requires deep explanation.

And there is deep explanation. The mechanics of the process organisms use to evolve from one form to another are increasingly understood. But the evidence for this is not dependent on in-depth scientific knowledge. I remember a number of years ago visiting the Burke Museum at the University of Washington. I was part of a group delivering some fossilized footprints that had been discovered at the two thousand foot level on the top of a mountain of forest owned by a client. The footprints were of a variety of animals including birds and mammals that had left their mark on the sand of the seashore some 50 million years earlier. One of the prints was of a small wolf, as I recall, with paw prints not much larger than a cat. I looked at this flat plate of stone that was once sand on a seashore that over millions of years had been pushed up to the top of the mountain. Looking at those prints and touching that rock filled me with a sense of awe and intimacy with the ancient days on this place we call home.

But I saw something else that struck me cold and made me question my basic belief in the way in which I understood God created his creatures. Hung from the ceiling of a room in the museum was the skeleton of a small whale, a beluga I believe. What amazed me was the skeleton of the fins. It looked like a human hand was attached without arm or wrist directly onto the side of the whale. All the fingers were there and even a sort of thumb. How could something so human-like be found on such a non-human-like creature?

Yes, it could be seen as the economy of design. Sort of like an engineer designing a car doesn't need to create a new device for steering the vehicle just because he is making a new model or even a completely different kind of vehicle. If it needs steering, the old idea of a steering wheel will work fine. Yes, that explanation has a certain ring to it. But the image of that hand on the whale also made it seem more plausible that variants of basic components could have developed over time based on their suitability for the environment in which they found themselves.

It is now safely beyond scientific dispute that life carries within itself the capability of adaptation. The process is incredibly complex and only partially understood. The role of quantum mechanics, whereby these processes ultimately start, is only beginning to be investigated.

Understanding the process of adaptation begins with unlocking the mystery of replication. How does one generation pass on its characteristics to the next generation? The understanding of replication was made possible by the work of such unlikely scientific heroes as Gregor Mendel, the Austrian monk who is considered one of the fathers of genetics. His work in crossbreeding peas helped to focus attention on the gene as the information-carrying device that enabled one kind of pea to pass its unique characteristics onto its descendants. The big breakthrough, of course, was the discovery of DNA. This double helix ladder of chemical elements provided a code that was unique to every individual.

Deoxyribonucleic acid (DNA) was first isolated by a Swiss doctor in 1869, but the famous double helix structure was identified in 1953 by James Watson and Francis Crick. This is arguably one of the greatest scientific discoveries of the past hundred years and has led to an explosion of understanding how life processes work. It's both remarkably simple and unimaginably complex. There are four basic substances called nucleotides, shortened to four letters: G, A, T and C. The combination of those four substances represents a code that defines the individual whether it be a single-celled animal or a human being. Every cell in the living entity contains the same DNA code. The double-helix structure enables it to split and reassemble thereby keeping the code intact (usually) as the living entity grows and cells divide.

Darwin's unique contribution was not to further the understanding of how life was reproduced, but how it changed as a result of the individuals encountering their environment. Looking at the finches he found on the Galapagos Islands while on the famous voyage of the Beagle completed in 1836, he noted the similarity of the birds to those found on the mainland.

Yet, their beaks were different and uniquely adapted to feeding on the nuts and seeds found on the island and not found on the mainland. How could it be that a bird could on its own, by moving to a new location, create a more suitable beak for itself?

Darwin was attuned to the Enlightenment spirit of the age, with major thinkers like Marquis De Laplace suggesting that Newton's discovery of the laws of motion and gravity meant that all nature could be understood if we just unlocked the laws that dictated how things happened. He was further influenced by a personal tragedy of the death of his young daughter and found he could no longer accept the idea of a loving, providential God. How could such a loving God have taken away his daughter? With a loss of faith, a keen scientific mind and the new thinking about the laws and mechanics of nature, he turned what he observed on this voyage into a rational explanation for how species could evolve.

The theory was simple. Random changes in individuals, be they trees or birds, occur in the process of replication from one generation to another. Most of those random and undirected changes are futile or even destructive to the unfortunate creature so afflicted. A frog with an extra toe is an oddball but has no advantage in surviving in a hostile environment. However, a frog that depends on licking bugs off leaves for his livelihood, has a definite advantage if he finds himself with an unusually long tongue. He can get more bugs more easily, can grow big and strong, can attract the most lovely and productive mates and in so doing pass on this strange new change onto the next generation. Randomly generated changes combined with natural selection based on "survival of the fittest," or those most well adapted to survive in the environment, are what Darwin's observations and theory is all about.

His explanations were much expanded by his defenders and advocates such as Thomas Huxley and Karl Marx. The ideas were almost immediately seized upon as the much-needed answer to William Paley's explanation of nature as evidence of design and a Designer—the famous watchmaker analogy. For the emerging evangelical atheists of this day such as Huxley, Darwin's ideas were, so to speak, a godsend. They provided the scientific "evidence" for what the progressive thinkers so much longed to believe which was that there was no need for the hypothesis of God to explain what we see in the natural world. Everything that couldn't be explained by gravity and the mechanical laws of classical physics could now be quite easily understood by these random changes creating ever newer and higher forms of life. It fit so well with the Enlightenment ideals not only of the primacy of man, but with the optimistic hope of a world made better or perfect through knowledge and a focus on humanity. The appeal of Darwin was not so much the startling science, but the adaptation of the science to the spirit of the age. When the student is ready, the saying goes, the teacher will come. The student was more than ready and Darwin the teacher dutifully showed up on time.

Soon, the idea of evolution jumped from the natural sciences to the emerging social sciences and Marx adopted its principles to attempt to explain the evolution of human history. August Compte took it to a new level creating a religion out of the "positive" era of human development to which evolution had led us. The lines were drawn, the battle was on and it has been raging for over 200 years.

This overly simplified narrative shows the importance of science, ideas, philosophy, politics combining in ways that determine culture, values and worldviews for millions of citizens of the world. But the essential question here is: what is true? Does Darwin's explanation and all the scientific work based on that give the necessary explanation for the immense variety of life on this planet? More importantly, can Darwin's ideas account for the very formation of life itself? If so, what are the implications for someone who is a theist? Does believing in the theory of evolution eliminate a rational belief in God and does it completely and irreversibly contradict the Biblical account of the creation of the world including man?

The anti-religion crusaders would have the world believe that anyone who is a Christian or a theist is irrational because one cannot, in their view, accept the well-founded tenets of evolution and still believe in God. It may come as a surprise to them as much as to much of the conservative Christian world that there are large number of thinking Christians who fully accept the established facts of evolution. One of the most prominent in the United States is Francis S. Collins. A highly respected scientist who headed the Human Genome Project, Collins was appointed by President Obama as head of the National Institutes of Health in 2009. Prior to that, in 2006 he wrote a highly regarded book called *The Language of God*. He also founded the organization BioLogos which has become a central place for exploration of theism and evolutionary science. A conservative, evangelical Christian, he carefully explained why he could both be a believer in the God of the Bible, including in Jesus as the revealed Son of God, and be a scientist in good standing who thoroughly accepts the findings of evolution.

But it is the British scientist/theologians who have contributed by far the most to this question of the conflict between science and faith including the science of evolution. These include Ian Barbour, Arthur Peacocke, John Polkinghorne, and Alister McGrath. Oxford Professor Keith Ward, while not a scientist, has also written extensively on these topics. Another prominent writer is theoretical physicist Paul Davies who, while making clear he subscribes to no traditional theistic or orthodox faith, consistently exposes the fallacy of those in the mechanistic or naturalistic mode who boldly claim that science has discounted fully the rationality of belief in a God of religion.

Those who take science seriously and who also take God seriously do not doubt what two hundred years of scientific inquiry into evolution have shown us. Evolution is more than a theory. While it does not have the mathematical clarity of classical physics, its fundamental processes have become increasingly exposed. A thinking Christian who denies this fact is similar to one who says that the age of the earth and universe is only an illusion. In other words, when all the evidence shows that geologic formations on the earth make it clear that the earth was formed about 4 billion years ago, those who cling to the young earth idea of creation are forced to conclude that either the tests and analysis are completely wrong or that God created earth with the virtually fool-proof appearance of age. I've heard very smart and very well educated Christians argue exactly this. But I've never heard an argument that I could accept as to why God would be such a joker or deceiver. It doesn't seem in the nature of the Creator God presented in the very Bible they seem to be trying so desperately to defend.

While Darwin and many who followed him were careful about the claims they made about how far evolution went, there are a number of voices in science today who are more and more stridently claiming that evolution provides the whole explanation. In other words, that evolutionary science goes far beyond explaining speciation, or the creation of the wide variety of different plants and animals we see, it also explains how life came to be. While there have been a number of theories of biogenesis presented, no one has been able to demonstrate the validity of those theories. We still have the question of how life began even if we accept to the fullest extent that evolution explains how life evolved after it began. Is this idea that science hasn't yet proven that life can generate spontaneously from the primordial elements of a planet like earth the last, best hope for those who cling to the idea of a creator God? If we say yes, and truthfully, that has been my tendency, we are subscribing to the "God of the gaps"—the very idea that has so exorcised non-theistic scientists for the past two hundred years. In other words, we believe in God because science hasn't come up with an explanation for some mystery—yet. Profound mysteries in nature still exist. But "God of the gaps" is like my old childish explanation for thunder—God rearranging the furniture in heaven. I couldn't understand what thunder was so it must be God doing something up there and it sure sounded like rearranging the furniture on an upper floor. But, if my faith in God hinges on this "proof" and I find out that there is a rational, natural explanation for that loud noise in the sky, then my faith disappears. In this view, the poor believer is left with less and less to hang onto as science provides more and more explanation for the deepest mysteries of the universe. The theist's belief has been weakened as fingers torn from a branch hanging over an endless chasm. The creation of life is the last finger in this scenario. Seen in this way, those eager to pry that last finger loose are moving far ahead of the science in declaring what evolution has proved and what is yet to be shown.

The reaction of the serious scientists who are also serious believers is to be very, very careful about this God of the gaps problem. So they say while science has not established biogenesis, or the spontaneous creation of life, it might be possible. The proof may come yet. We are waiting for experiments that validate the theories. They may come, they may not, but as long as there are scientists, they will search for the proof. And if that proof finally does come, those theistic scientists do not see a need for their faith to go the way of the dodo. In other words, they are not pinning their belief in a creator God on the fact that there is still no proof for spontaneous creation of life. How can that be? Wouldn't proof of biogenesis be the death knell of belief?

No. I focus on this issue because it goes to the root of the matter, and also shows why it is very possible and rational for someone to believe in the traditional God of religion and still fully accept the proven facts of evolution. Let's explore how it is possible to believe that life evolved spontaneously and still believe in a Creator.

Stars are born and die. Planets accumulate mass from clouds of dust and matter and begin their life orbiting around a star that will someday collapse and die. Explosions of dying stars spew material into the universe that collects under the force of gravity to form these planets and further provide the material needed for this mysterious, miraculous thing called life. All that we see now clearly is a process, or system, or machine that runs according to some reasonably well known laws of classical physics. Before we might have believed that each star in the sky was placed there by the hand of God, that each planet was carefully constructed by gigantic hands, and each molecule of carbon from a dying star guided to its destination in my brain by a loving God intimately involved in every act, every interaction, every part of anything that went on in his universe. Now, we know that these things may involve the providence of God, a subject we will explore further, but they may also occur completely on their own based on the laws of nature.

We have learned that these laws are quite spectacular in their precision. We can call it a very lucky coincidence or we can call it design, but there is little ground in between. It is rational to accept either idea, despite what the evangelists for naturalism might say. Where did these laws come from? The greatest miracle of the universe, thought Einstein was the rationality of the universe and our capability as humans to understand that rationality. David Lindley states "[Einstein] began to marvel that it is possible to do science at all, expressing his puzzlement at one time by saying, 'The world of our sense experience is comprehensible. The fact that it is comprehensible is a miracle.'"

The greatest evidence for the Creator God according to Polkinghorne is the fundamental beauty and rationality of these laws. The fact that we can apprehend these even darkly is one of our best indications that we were made by the One who created these laws specifically to understand, worship and enter into relationship. The laws we have discovered over the past few hundred years have made it clear that we live in a universe with the inherent capability to make itself. God, in this view, is not so much the Creator of the individual stars, but of a most magnificent star-making machine. And galaxy-making machine. And carbon-making machine. And planet-making machine.

Could it be, can it be, that this God is also the maker of a life-making machine? Looking at it this way it is clear how the

Collins' and Polkinghornes' and their like can be quite comfortable with the idea of biogenesis—even though it is very far from proven. So what if it is? We still go back to the question, how did these laws and these processes that made the spontaneous creation of life possible come into being. Coincidence or design? Random luck, or an act of intelligence and will? And how is it that we mortals, evolved as we have from stardust, have the ability to comprehend this mysterious universe? This is no longer a God of the gaps issue. The only gap left to answer is who created the laws, the process, the fine-tuning and how do we understand the miracle of comprehensibility? Again we come to the simple choice of chance or design, both requiring faith and both rational explanations for the greatest mystery of all.

Given that, let's look at what evolution proves and what it doesn't prove given today's state of knowledge. Paul Davies in his book *The 5th Miracle* states the situation clearly:

"How did something so immensely complicated, so finessed, so exquisitely clever, come into being all on its own? How can mindless molecules, capable only of pushing and pulling their immediate neighbors, cooperate to form and sustain something as ingenious as a living organism?...Few scientists believe that life began in a single monumental leap. No physical process abruptly 'breathed life' into inert matter. There must have been a long and complicated transitional stage between the nonliving and the first truly living thing, an extended chronology of events unlikely to be preordained in its myriad details. A law of nature could not alone explain how life began, because no conceivable law would compel a legion of atoms to follow precisely a prescribed sequence of assemblage."

Francis Collins, former head of the Human Genome Project who we introduced earlier, in *The Language of God* writes:

"But how did self-replicating organisms arise in the first place? It is fair to say that at the present time we simply do not know. No current hypothesis comes close to explaining how in the space of a mere 150 million years, the pre-biotic environment that existed on planet Earth gave rise to life. That is not to say that reasonable hypotheses have not been put forward, but their statistical probability of accounting for the development of life still seems remote."

If you are a theist and draw a big sigh of relief from these words from an eminent scientist, Collins would urge you to great caution. He quickly goes on to state:

"A word of caution is needed when inserting specific divine action by God in this or any other area where scientific understanding is currently lacking. From solar eclipses in olden times to the movement of the planets in the Middle Ages, to the origins of life today, this "God of the gaps" approach has all too often done a disservice to religion (and by implication, to God, if that's possible). Faith that places God in the gaps of current understanding about the natural world may be headed for crisis if advances in science subsequently fill those gaps. Faced with an incomplete understanding of the natural world, believers should be cautious about invoking the divine in areas of current mystery, lest they build an unnecessary theological argument that is doomed to later destruction."

Collins rejects the God of the gaps arguments but believes there are powerful reasons to believe in God based on what is known rather than what is unknown. In this way he is in agreement with Polkinghorne and so many of the other scientist/theologians who have dealt seriously with this topic.

"There are good reasons to believe in God, including the existence of mathematical principles and order in creation. They are positive reasons, based on knowledge, rather than default assumptions based on (a temporary) lack of knowledge."

When confronting the facts of evolution, the non-theist concludes that mere chance, blind chance as the preferred phrase has it today, is responsible for the origin of life and the way life evolved into conscious beings capable of understanding the processes that created them. The theist has two alternatives in accepting these facts. The one is that the Creator made a machine with the mechanism in place whereby the universe could make itself including life and that life then could take a direction on its own consistent with the operating instructions of that machine. Or the theist could say that the Creator made a machine that allowed him the opportunity to tinker and be involved with the process of making. This idea, referred to as *creatio continua* means that creation is not a single act of the Creator but something that continues with active involvement to this day. If this is true then the question becomes how God uses the machine he created to manage the development process. To understand that, we need to look at the big issue of chance and necessity.

You might say that life is like a game of cards. Without rules there can be no game. But the way the cards are shuffled is a matter of chance. Evolution requires both strict, unbreakable rules and the luck of the draw. The highly predictable replication process made possible by DNA and RNA is matched by the very occasional uncertainty introduced by mutations. Without the rules of replication, there could be no continuity from one generation to the next. Without the occasional mutation or minor disruption of that replication, there could be no evolution or change.

Jacques Monod, a Nobel prize-winning French biologist, wrote about this balance in a famous book called *Chance and Necessity*. He believed that life resulted from a freak chemical accident that was such a wild piece of luck that it is highly unlikely to have occurred or will occur anywhere else in the universe. Monod was also an esteemed philosopher of science and concluded that, "Man at last knows he is alone in the unfeeling immensity of the universe, out of which he has emerged only by chance."

It is virtually impossible to avoid the conclusion of the ultimate meaninglessness of life and our existence if everything is explained by blind chance and inexplicable rules. As Polkinghorne states in explaining the conclusions of atheist biologists:

"The aptness of living creatures to their environment seems not to be the result of skillful design but of painful trial and error. Beneath it all lie simply the operations of chance, random mutations that are mostly deleterious but occasionally, by accident, produce a winning ticket in the lottery of life. Humans may rejoice in nature, but ultimately it is a tale told by an idiot, full of sound and fury, signifying nothing. This is the bleak picture painted for us by atheist biologists such as Jacques Monod and Richard Dawkins."

If life is more than a tale told by an idiot, if our ability to comprehend and experience wonder and awe at the natural world and our place in it means anything, then there must be a role for God somewhere in this grand spectacle of self-creating life. An intuition that is virtually universal in all of human existence is that there is meaning and purpose and therefore there is God. That intuition is expressed in the prayers of every human being—the inherent tendency we share to seek help from a power much greater than ourselves in our most desperate need as well as the tendency to lift our eyes, hearts and hands high in a desire to communicate the joy and gratitude and exaltation we experience at least occasionally in this life.

All evolutionists whether of the theist or atheist variety understand that life has evolved according to chance and necessity. Both are required. The laws are necessary to provide a reliable, predictable means for life to evolve. But if there were only rigid laws and no change, there could be no mutation, no natural selection, no adaptation to a challenging environment. Within both the laws and the "random" changes lie opportunities for God to participate in the process of continuing creation.

Polkinghorne has argued, as have others, that even within the self-making world, there seems to be a sense of direction or momentum that while not being overly restrictive or prescriptive suggests there is an inherent bias built into the very nature of the universe and the laws that make evolution possible. Polkinghorne describes it as a mountain range with valleys through which a stream passes. The stream coming from the higher reaches of the range is the stream of evolution. It has a certain freedom to flow where it will; there is no set bed for the creeks and rivers to flow. And yet the shape of the ridges, gullies and valleys determine that flow to some degree. Ultimately, the features of the range determine that a conscious being with the intelligence to understand its environment and manipulate it to some degree is inevitable. The specific shape of and characteristics of that being may not be pre-determined, but the fact of its emergence and its essential nature may be.

The Cambridge paleontologist Simon Conway-Morris, also believes evolution isn't as accidental or random as one might suspect. According to Shelly Emling, author of *The Fossil Hunter*, the professor believes if evolution began all over again, human intelligence would develop pretty much in the same way as it has. Conway-Morris emphasizes that developments happen as a result of pre-existing conditions, such as the need for blood cells to have hemoglobin in order to transport oxygen. Evolution, therefore, works only because it plays out within a certain set of rules.

Emling quotes Conway-Morris: "Evolution 'is after all only a mechanism, but if evolution is predictive, indeed possesses a logic, then evidently it is being governed by deeper principles,' he recently wrote. 'Come to think about it so are all sciences; why should Darwinism be any exception?'"

Similar to those who fiercely claim that fine-tuning is a merely a most astounding coincidence, those who also fiercely claim that evolution does away with God must answer the question as to why the process of evolution seems so clearly directed at what we now observe the current outcome to be. In the very laws or processes that make the rich variety of life possible, and make it possible for us to speak of a self-creating universe, we see the distinct possibility of intention or intelligent will at work.

Perhaps the laws reflect God's intention for life, but what about chance? Is there not also the possibility, if not the likelihood, of God's continuing involvement in the on-going work of evolution or creation? Is God still in his workshop tinkering with the quarks and leptons, the molecules and their arrangements that will enable future species to adapt fruitfully to the environments they may find themselves in? The question goes back to the uncertainty principle and chaos theory. We have seen how even the most minor shifts of energy in an electron, the change in its orbit around the nucleus, can affect massive change in complex systems. We have further discussed how these changes are seen as fuzzy, unpredictable and to a large degree unobservable. Whether the spin of one particle flips this way or that, requiring the spin of its entangled pair to flip the other way on the other side of the universe, is seen as random. But what physicist can say with certainty that what appears to be random is actually random, that the result is completely uninfluenced or directed, completely free of any intention or will? Calling it random versus an intentional act of an unknown will is a metaphysical conclusion, not a provable scientific statement.

While such possibility entices us with the opportunity for a divine will to participate in the on-going and thoroughly natural process of evolution, a stern caution is in order. We must remember Aunt Shirley's cancer. If we believe that God has the power and the right to adjust the particles and molecules that underlie her disease, can we easily avoid the question as to why she had to suffer from it in the first place? If we conclude that the beauty we revel in of the creation of Adam and Eve, or of the magnificent wildcat that runs across the African savannah, is the work of a loving Creator, how do we answer those critics who say that this same beneficent will could have prevented the Holocaust, the terror attacks, the horrendous mutilation of innocent children? This same God who made the cat also made it to attack and eat the gazelle who also runs beautifully across that picturesque grassland. How can we reconcile these pictures?

The devastating impact of that question is no doubt what drives many thinking, caring human beings to retreat into the relative comfort of leaving it all to chance. Even the laws by which evolution is possible emerged from the chaos by chance. It is an understandable position, but still an intellectual retreat. Atheism, it turns out, may be a form of escape, a way out of the most difficult questions--an opiate for the masses.

Chapter 6
Information: Foundation and Immortality

In my adult life, I have witnessed -- and participated in to some degree -- the evolution of one of the most powerful creations of humankind and how it came to dominate, manage and largely control our lives. I'm talking about software.

As I write these words, once again about seven miles above the earth, I am amazed as I think about this massive machine carrying me and another hundred or so passengers across the continent. In the cockpit are two pilots but they have become to some degree superfluous. The "glass cockpit" of a modern passenger plane has the capability of flying itself. A destination can be programmed in and the plane can take off, despite even severe weather conditions, and land on its own—avoiding air traffic and thunderstorms in its path—at its intended destination. It is all done by very clever combinations of two digits—zeros and ones.

In 1979 I was a university professor, teaching drama, communications and fine arts. I left the teaching world to become a partner in a software startup. I had no idea what a computer was or what software looked like. As an arts person I had an instinctive dislike for computers, I suppose because they tended to reside at that time in the math and science departments and we artsy types had a certain disdain for the "pocket protector" set. But, an intriguing opportunity lurked, so I went to the university bookstore and bought the introductory text on computers. That's where I learned what software was and how software and hardware interacted to produce the results we called computation.

A few months later I was chatting with one my partners who was starting this venture and who had spent the last couple of years programming a business application. We were setting up shop to sell that application. He looked at the large box sitting in our cramped office that was a brand new IBM System 34—the hottest mid-range computer at that time. Inside the box, somewhere amidst all the wires and circuits and components, was the software he created. "There's a cathedral in there," he commented with the pride of an architect and craftsman. He meant that while I couldn't see it or even begin to understand it, that what resided in that box was something of great value and even beauty. It was his art, his own creative expression; somehow his very spirit, he seemed to be saying, was captured in those bits and bytes running around those circuits in that big box.

Most people go through their daily lives without thinking much about how our lives have been transformed by software. We even tend to forget how almost everything we do and touch has been reduced to those two digits. When we send a text message on our smartphones, the little screen on our computer is representing a letter by a combination of ones and zeros. It takes combinations of eight bits to represent one letter. So an "L" might be 01110101. While an "O" might be 10111101. These eight bit combinations, also called bytes, can be used to represent all kinds of characters, the letters of the alphabet, numbers, operators and so on. So when you send a message to a friend that her text message was funny and you respond with LOL, the little computer in your hand is actually transmitting something like 01110101 10111101 01110101. Of course to transmit that message, that you are "laughing out loud" requires a number of instructions, but those instructions are also captured in zeros and ones. The program in your phone sends instructions to other programs in computers in the cell phone companies translating your LOL via an internet connection to radio waves carried by a complex network of cell towers, correctly identifying the intended recipient, translating the radio waves back into bits and bytes that can be interpreted by her smartphone and appear as a message on her tiny screen. She smiles, knowing that she has made you laugh and maybe brightened your day.

Suppose you snap a photo or shoot a video with your smartphone. Or suppose you decide you want to listen to a little classical musical while you do your pilates. In each case you would be sending messages consisting of those zeros and ones, which would further command an absolutely amazing complex sequence of almost perfectly precise zeros and ones that would capture your child playing on a swing, or capture perfectly the notes of a master violinist playing your favorite Mozart composition.

The volume of zeros and ones floating around our world and the power that is contained in them is almost incomprehensible. What makes it even more difficult to understand that this has all come about in the last twenty to thirty years.

The evolution of our digital world has resulted in a less obvious but important change in another way that is relevant to our discussion about the universe, life and ourselves. Information theory has entered the world of scientific understanding and is providing some valuable insights into how things work—particularly the science of evolution. It is profoundly affecting our understanding of the workings of brains and, perhaps, even of consciousness.

It isn't natural, is it, to think of a beautiful photograph as nothing more than a sequence of zeros and ones? Yet, almost all photography has gone digital. It doesn't seem intuitive to think when listening to Mozart on your headset that the rich tones filling your ears are nothing more than a complex sequence of zeros and ones. And neither is it natural to think of capturing the essence of that cheetah on the African plains as a very rich sequence of information. But that animal consists of carbon, and oxygen, and hydrogen—molecules and atoms that were once spewed as raw materials from the ash and dust from giant star explosions. In ways that are still mysterious but fall under our current understanding of evolution, these bits and pieces of matter are organized in some very precise ways. So much so that the cheetah is quite distinct not only from the gazelle it is chasing, but also from the baby cheetah which is the motivator of its intense hunt. It has a unique combination of molecules, atoms and quarks, interacting in unique ways. There is no other creature exactly like it and there never will be another exactly like it. Thinking of it in this way, is it conceivable to think of that unique combination being captured by information, even by bits and bytes or zeros and ones? Could quarks and electrons and nuclei be uniquely identified and represented in ways similar to how we capture, store and reproduce complex images and sounds? Could the genetic information that is so faithfully reproduced by chemical processes be reduced to digital data? Could the processes themselves be reduced to instructions similar to those found in complex computer programs?

I used to fantasize that I could envision a way of teleportation. This ability to move objects in space and time seems one of the last great frontiers of human endeavor. Now we can move information around the globe and even to distant parts of our visible universe at the speed of light. We can transmit photos of our grandkids or the first sounds of a new baby across the globe in seconds. We do it by reducing the patterns of light we see as letters on a page or colors in an image into an extremely long series of individual digits. Then we transmit those digits across the room, continent or deep into space. How might it be possible to transmit an object? An object like a rock is made up of atoms and molecules that are readily available almost anywhere on the earth we can imagine. So are people for that matter. Mostly H_2O, some carbon, some protein, etc. These can be found almost anywhere. So, if I could reduce the very specific sequence of how these particles are arranged into bits and bytes, isn't it conceivable that I could make a machine that could use those instructions to assemble the molecules and atoms in just the right way so that I could appear anywhere the program I created directed? The emergence of 3D printers that literally assemble copies of objects by building them up from little particles suggests that this may be possible at some point. Of course, to not cause some serious problems in the universe I would have to not only reassemble those pieces of matter according to the very precise sequence that I transmitted, I would also have to simultaneously disassemble the pieces here. Otherwise I wouldn't be teleporting, I would be cloning or duplicating and then the world would be populated by rocks or humans that were precisely the same but operating in different parts of the universe. That just doesn't seem quite right.

I take you on this wandering trail of fantasy in order to introduce the idea of information. Increasingly, it seems, scientists are applying information theory to some of the great mysteries of nature and life. And perhaps coincidentally, perhaps not, theologians are also looking at information theory as explanations for some of the dark mysteries of belief, including the idea of resurrection.

Paul Davies, for one, looks at information theory as a means of shedding light on the formation of life. Information processing consists of three different elements. There is the data, the programming and the hardware. All three are needed to do anything useful. For example, if you want a computer to do a simple computation, say you want the computer to produce a result by multiplying 3 times 9, you need all three elements. The three and the nine are your data. You need a program that tells the little logic gates in the hardware what to do when they encounter the eight bit sequences of zeros and ones that represent the numbers. And you need those logic gates wired to an input device so you can input the data and the program and an output device so you can see or record the result.

Ray Kurzweil is one of our more intriguing technologists and thinkers of this generation. Despite a diverse career, a primary focus has been recognizing patterns. In other words, information. His first major invention to bring him national recognition was a reading machine that used optical character recognition to scan text and then read it aloud so that blind people could access books and text. From text recognition, he moved to speech recognition and the Siri application so popular on iphones is a result of his research and development work on recognizing the patterns of human speech. His book *How to Create a Mind: The Secret of Human Thought Revealed*, builds on this work by demonstrating that the brain is essentially a pattern recognition machine. Experiences, thoughts and memories are all patterns recorded and transmitted in electrical impulses and minute chemical changes emerging from a cells networked in an exceedingly complex hierarchy. His and other pioneering artificial intelligence technologists operate on the understanding that all thought, including consciousness, is information. That is, it consists of patterns which can be captured, stored, blended with others, and replayed.

Kurzweil and others in the field of artificial intelligence are promoting the idea that consciousness emerges as a natural evolutionary process from the complexity of the patterns. This idea has been grabbed onto by evangelical atheists such as Daniel Dennett who aggressively promote the idea of emergent consciousness. But, there is a problem here. A problem we'll call meaning.

Even if you conclude that there is a vast program that is determining how the particles, atoms and molecules that emerged from star dust came together to form life and, over time, all the varieties of life, there is something else that escapes this thought: meaning. Information is not meaning. But information can mean something if someone is capable of understanding that meaning.

Words on a page are information. That is true whether those words are typed by William Shakespeare or a room full of monkeys. In fact, if that famous room full of monkeys typed out the exact words of a Shakespearean sonnet, the information would be precisely the same. But those words mean something to Shakespeare as they mean something to most people capable of reading English. They don't mean much to the monkeys. To a reader of Chinese or Arabic, the marks on the page would be as meaningful as information to the monkeys. How can a few marks on a page, or for that matter a precise series of zeroes and ones, bring us to tears, make our hearts rise with joy, or bring back memories of delight or terror?

The distinction is clear when thinking of computers vs. people. Computers can process vast amounts of information. Even those we now carry around in our pockets and purses can turn so many of those zeros and ones into other zeros and ones in precise and accurate sequences that we begin to lose track of the magnitude of the task they are performing. When I began selling software in 1980, the machine that ran our software had 128 megabytes of memory, was the size and weight of a compact car, heated up a whole office with its processing, and cost over $100,000. To translate those 128 megabytes into our zeros and ones, a byte was eight bits with a bit being a single digit either a zero or one. Mega is a million, so it means that the IBM System 34 could hold an astounding 128 million sets of eight bit characters in its RAM or random access memory at one time. As I write this the newest smartphones come with 16 gigabytes of storage. That is sixteen thousand billion combinations of that series of eight individual digits -- in your pocket or purse!

Even this vast processing power pales in comparison with the processing power of the human brain. Kurzweil focuses on the neocortex and reports that in this "new brain" (meaning evolved later in more intelligent life) there are 30 billion neurons, or brain cells. But these neurons are connected together into something called "pattern recognizers," and there are 300 million of these pattern recognizers in the neocortex.

But of far greater importance than the sheer amount of data that can be processed is the incredibly important distinction between information and meaning. Computers can process data but they cannot derive meaning from the data. This dividing line was explored in the famous 1968 Stanley Kubrick film 2001: A Space Odyssey when the computer named Dave took over the spaceship. Even then, the question remains whether as a computer Dave was programmed to simulate an ability to interpret data and act independently on it or whether or not he had actually crossed the line into consciousness.

Computers can certainly be made to look like they can derive meaning from information but that ability has to be imputed to them, in other words, it has to come from the outside, from someone who does really have the capability of interpreting information and taking independent action based on it. Let's say I open a letter addressed to me that says, "Dial 75230 on your cell phone before 6 pm tonight or you will be killed." If that message had been written in Chinese, I would recognize it as information, that is symbols and patterns on a page, but I would derive no meaning from it and I would therefore not take any action based on the information. I could program a computer to recognize those symbols in English or Chinese and to take the action of dialing the correct digits thereby saving my life. That does not mean the computer understood the message and the meaning it had for me. The meaning remained with me. It was I interpreting the information in advance and taking action through the computer.

Most of us follow our intuition in understanding that there is something in the world called will and action. The old mechanists of yesterday could not deal with it and indeed many in science today who are fully committed to the concept of a closed, deterministic and mechanistic system have great trouble accepting the idea of free will and independent, free and meaningful action. In fact, meaning doesn't really mean much in a fully mechanistic world. Keith Ward, an Oxford philosopher of impressive credentials who became the Regius Professor of Divinity at Oxford, has written extensively on this issue of action and freedom. It is at this precise point where the paths of theism and atheism diverge when looking at the question from a scientific perspective. Because if there is no meaning, then all is information and there is only the appearance of meaning. It means that our brains are indeed computers made of meat and that what appears to us to be our freedom to choose is nothing more than blind slavery to what has already been programmed into us by our genes and the chemical and quantum reactions that represent the sum total of our existence. You cannot really accept the idea that there is meaning that escapes the containment of our quarks, gluons and as yet unknown particles, and remain true to the "there can be no God" argument. Meaning is not something that evolves as much as the committed atheists would try to make it.

In fact, the lack of meaning and ultimately the lack of rationality in the naturalistic scheme presents an ultimate "defeater" argument to the idea of naturalism. The argument against theism is based on rational logic presented by naturalists who are operating deterministically from a basis that says rationality is an illusion. Our thoughts and ideas are simply an illusion because they proceed from a senseless, meaningless system of laws. Rational thinking in an atheistic, mechanistic world is an oxymoron. How can such arguments be taken seriously? This understanding is much more cogently and comprehensively developed by the highly regarded philosopher, Alvin Plantinga, particularly in his book *Where the Conflict Really Lies.*

Who are you, really? Are you ultimately information? And what about immortality--how is it you could live beyond this life? Aren't you as you are known by yourself and those closest to you a combination of your personality, your physical traits, your experiences, your education, your memories? Many of these you inherited from your parents, but much of who you are is uniquely your own, born of your circumstances in life and of the choices you have made. When you think of it, we are a combination of genetic information and experiential information. The genetic information is contained in every cell of our bodies. The experiential information, which we'll just refer to as memory, is also stored as information, in our specialized memory cells in our brains.

Now you will understand a little why I took you on that meandering journey through my own experience of encountering information. Let's look at the miracle of DNA and genetic replication as information. DNA contains a very small number of chemical substances called nucleotides. There are just four of them, twice as many as our binary system of ones and zeros. Those four chemical substances go by the letters G, A, T and C. No need to give you the chemical names they stand for as you can go to Wikipedia yourself for that. In a process that today remains largely mysterious, the genetic code is passed on by instructions that assemble the chemicals in the cell in a very, very, very precise order. The famous double helix, or twisted ladder shape of the DNA molecule contains the sequence of these proteins that tell the rest of the organism everything it needs to know to operate. My DNA is similar to yours, but profoundly different. It's what makes us unique individuals. DNA is a set of instructions, a pattern, a code. Instead of using zeros and ones to store the details and pass on instructions, it stores it as those four distinct proteins. But, it isn't too hard to imagine that those proteins could be reinterpreted as zeros and ones, or any other form of storing and conveying information we choose. DNA and our genetic code is information stored as chemicals. But, it is information pure and simple.

What about memories? Our brains remain a great mystery, despite having learned much in the past few years. We know that our brains are made of a special kind of cell called neurons along with other support cells. The neurons interact chemically and electrically with each other, passing tiny particles of vital information between each other through small gaps called synapses. Minutest electrical charges stimulate this interchange. A single interaction or conveyance of chemicals between two neurons conveys little information, but when connected together in a pattern involving a number of them, information can be stored and conveyed. Just like a single zero or one is empty of content, a precise pattern of synapses can convey complex information and meaning. It is the pattern of interactions between neurons that holds the secret to how our brain functions and specifically how memory works.

Ray Kurzweil's work on artificial intelligence is based on a fundamental understanding of these wet cells in the brain working in tandem as "pattern recognizers." The complexity of our experiences and memories is captured in hierarchies of these pattern recognizers. Each pattern recognizer module contains a number of cells specially tasked to fire when that particular pattern is called for by the control center of the brain. For example, when you think of the letter "T" there are pattern recognizers assigned to the upper bar and others assigned to the lower bar and they are called to fire in recalling that particular graphic element. The speed and fluidity of brain processing is based largely on the capability to predict which patterns are needed in advance of them being needed, as well as inhibitory signals to other pattern recognizers telling them they are not needed for a particular task or recollection.

When you suddenly smell something that returns you instantly to warm and delightful memories of your mother cooking a favorite meal in your childhood kitchen, that smell came into your brain through olfactory nerves that picked up chemicals in the air. The electrical impulses from the olfactory nerves were sent up to a processing center in your brain that triggered the pattern recognizer modules related to the olfactory nerves to light up. They light up like a pattern of lights on a dark skyscraper at night. The pattern was similar to (but never quite the same as) the pattern of neurons that was created by your experience of your mother, the food, a warm and safe place, the hunger you felt, the anticipation of a wonderful meal, and the love and appreciation you experienced. All that was captured in a vast, but very specific and precise set of electro-chemical interactions. The smell triggered that sequence and when the sequence was picked up by your brain's processing center, you re-experienced the emotions, recalled the images, and sighed in delight and nostalgia.

If the electrical impulses that capture, store and convey this are in effect numerical information, cannot they also be captured in the form of ones and zeros? Theoretically, yes. They are "merely" information. The lights and darks and multiple colors of a digital print are an information representation of the sunset scene or bowl of fruit. The ones and zeros stored on your CD or your music-playing smart phone precisely capture the rich, complex sounds of the orchestra or rock band. It is a stretch, but not an impossible one, to think of all our memories, experiences, emotions and all of our lives being captured, stored, transmitted, and replayed as information.

What happens to your memories when you die? You know that these memories exist in your brain and your brain is made of living tissue requiring food including oxygen. When tissue dies, it returns to the basic forms of stardust from which it emerged: carbon, hydrogen, oxygen, etc. There is no capacity in dead tissue to store electrical impulses or to control when those complex patterns might reappear. Memory dies with the body, or so it would seem. Our mind rebels against this thought. I would not remember my own name after death? I would not recognize the face of my husband or wife or children? I would have no sensation of past joys? Then what good is life after death? Indeed. If all memories die with death, we might as well give up on the idea of life after death entirely. The very idea of immortality is based on the idea of preserving who we really are, and that means preserving what we have learned and experienced as well as what we have received by genetic gift. It means our memories cannot die if we are to live.

Belief in immortality, a continuation of our selves beyond death, is deeply ingrained in who we are as human beings. Death is the intruder, we sense. Death is the unnatural part of our existence. Death does not belong here. We rebel against any idea that dying is just the way it is and the way it should be. But, if we have any sense of a meaningful life after death, we have to have a sense of how those unique patterns of information that define who we are can survive the destruction of our bodies.

The answer is in understanding our memories as information. This requires thinking about them in terms of those three elements: data, programming and hardware. What is the data in this picture? The synapses, particularly the pattern of them that represents a specific memory. What is the program? Using Kurzweil's model, it is the instructions used to direct the firing of all the various pattern recognizers to recall a specific memory -- instructions themselves contained in other patterns of synapses. What is the hardware? The wet cells, electrons, chemicals, atoms, molecules and elemental particles that are called your brain.

To the pure mechanist, memory is a very physical if highly complex process that is dependent on writing the code and storing the data using the hardware (your brain and body) that is needed to run the program and exhibit the result. In this very physical view, there can be no question that memory dies with you. The patterns or codes that represent your memories are inextricably tied to your hardware. Your brain cells die. The pattern of synapses that trigger the recall dies with it. That can only mean that all of you, every bit that is you—your heredity, your personality, your memories, your original thoughts—everything that makes you you of necessity must die when you breathe your last breath. Unless, a huge unless, the record of those patterns is somehow kept. Unless the information is stored or moved to some other "hardware."

One of the major innovations in computer processing that is being implemented today is something called "cloud computing." In the last few years we have been rapidly moving from the early days of software where data and programming first resided on very large computers called mainframes. Then, starting in the early 1980s, it was distributed to lots of desktop computers that were typically called PCs or personal computers. The data and programming used to run the computers were kept mostly with the computer itself. Not any more. Now the software is much more distributed. Mobile or smart phones are loaded with software, yet most of the software that makes them so powerful does not reside in that little device in your pocket. It resides on servers—large networks of computers—that are themselves kept in large "server farms" or data centers. These centers hold many thousands of very powerful servers and deliver the data and programming instructions out to your computer devices by way of networks. The networks used to be mostly private where companies or organizations would be wired together through phone lines, fiber cables, satellite connections, microwave systems, and so on. But now by far the most significant network is the Internet. Where is the Internet? There is no one location, it is all over the world. The Internet consists of servers all over the world interconnected with a vast array of instructions that pass data and instructions to each other by some means of connection: phone lines, fiber cable, satellite, radio, etc. In fact, there are systems on the Internet that make use of the processing power held by individuals in their own desktop or laptop computers. One of the biggest processing challenges on the Internet, the SETI project, or the search for intelligent life in the universe, harnesses the computer processing power of millions of individual personal computers.

Today, you can still maybe locate at least some of the data and some of the programming instructions you may use as part of your work or home life on individual servers on the Internet. Web-based applications may be run from multiple server farms or data centers in order to provide backup or redundancy—if one server farm goes down or gets blown up, another is programmed to take over for it without anyone likely noticing. But cloud computing takes this idea of dispersed data and programming much further. It harnesses the power of multiple data centers in a way that promises to significantly enhance processing power, data storage, and reliability. With cloud computing, the data related to an email you send or a video of your cute child may be widely separated. Some of it could be located in servers or routers located in southern Texas, while other parts of that data could at the same time be located (for an instant perhaps) in a connection in Russia or Puerto Rico. Where is it? In the "cloud."

With this in mind, it is not such a stretch to think that the very precise pattern of your memories may be stored some place other than your own hardware. Thinking of it as limited to my own personal PC, or PB (personal brain) is really an outdated way of thinking about information and processing. Like today's software, where it actually resides is probably just about impossible to tell and completely irrelevant. What is important is that I can recall the data I want using the specific instructions I want when and how I want it. In other words, I don't care where the names and numbers on my phone list are stored—they can be in the clouds for all I care. I just want to be able to find them quickly when I need them either using my computer at home or in the office or using my little computer in my pocket if that is more convenient.

Polkinghorne makes the analogy of software and hardware when dealing with the very significant issue of brain and mind, soul and body. He points out that the duality between soul and body that we in the Western world and in the Christian world have come to accept as reality is a Greek construction. It is not representative of Jewish thinking and it is not in reality biblical. In fact, it leads us to some common conclusions that may contradict biblical teaching. He argues instead for something he calls "dual aspect monism." By dual aspect he means that there are two parts to our existence as human beings—our mind or consciousness and our bodies. By "monism" he means that in fact the two are inseparable. Our memories are not possible without the brain cells that are triggered by the patterns that are in themselves stored in our brains. Our emotions cannot exist outside of the complex electrical and chemical reactions in our brains that also interact with our hormones and muscles. But our hardware wears out. It weakens and eventually dies. And that would suggest that all those patterns—both the patterns that can be considered the precise information about who we are and the patterns that represent our personalities and memories—these too disappear with the death of the hardware. Unless, the information also operates in the cloud. If it happens that the programming and the data that makes us who we are is not lost but is preserved somewhere in some vast cloud of servers, it would not be unreasonable to consider that cloud the Mind of God. And that is exactly what Polkinghorne suggests.

If this might actually be the case, it sheds a different light on the concept of resurrection. Suppose for a moment that all your memories were retained as information, data and programming, in the "cloud" we'll call the Mind of God. While there, it can do nothing because it has no associated hardware. No additional information can be captured. It cannot even be "processed" in the sense we understand processing, such as recalling a memory, because processing requires a processor and that is hardware. Data and programming can only be stored if it is not accessed by some input, output and processing capability of hardware. Software needs to be tied to some sort of keyboard or screen or microphone, push button or touch pad—some kind of controlling and responding device to make it do anything and mean anything. It needs hardware and so do human beings. We do not exist and cannot be imagined to exist without a way of expressing the information and coding that makes us. Resurrection in this view is a hardware upgrade. Hopefully, a new and improved model, one that will make the data and programming operate to its full potential. And hopefully one that is infinitely upgradeable so that we can look forward to a non-stop process of adding to the software, the memories and experiences, that we take into our new bodies.

It is interesting with this in mind, that one of the most respected theologians and biblical scholars of our time, N. T. Wright, has written extensively on how most of the Christian world misunderstands the biblical teaching on life after death. If you were to ask most people, Christian or not, where they go after death most Americans would say that the good go to heaven. An orthodox Christian would say that those who believe in Jesus Christ and have been saved by his sacrificial death are the ones that go to heaven. But where is heaven? We have envisioned it as the abode of God and the angels and we have a very hard time getting over the picture of an elderly God in white beard surrounded by bright winged beings strumming quite beautifully on harps while floating weightlessly on clouds. We also believe that our souls go to heaven immediately upon death even while our bodies are rotting in the grave or have been reduced to ashes.

Not so, says Wright. He is quite clear in his teaching that what the Bible proclaims, the New Testament in particular, is life after life after death. The resurrection, modeled on the resurrection of Jesus, is an actual restoration of the physical bodies that we inhabited while on earth. It teaches that our home will not be in heaven but on a re-created new earth. Along with the reset button being used for earth, it will also be used on heaven as almost every reference to the new earth also references a new heaven. Presumably, since references to heaven typically refer to the "firmament" or up there, or that part of the universe that we see is away from us but largely unknown, presumably that means the reset button includes the universe. However, what we can be certain of based on this interpretation of the Bible, is that the upgrade in hardware that Polkinghorne refers to is based not on some airy-fairy musings of an elderly physicist, but on the most solid biblical thinking of our time. Further, both agree that the one and only resurrection event that humans have been witness to is the assurance of this promise and the best clue we have to what this upgrade will look like.

Of course, this raises the question of what happens to us when we die, or what about life after death and not just life after life after death? If there is anything real about resurrection we must know that in some way the patterns or programs, plus the data that make us uniquely who we are is preserved. If who we are is not stored in the Mind of God as Polkinghorne suggests, then certainly that data that makes us us must be retrieved from somewhere to be reinstalled in the resurrected hardware. Whether that storage process includes conscious awareness and of a sense of time passing, I could not say. My inclination would be that the storage occurs without consciousness so that while we may exist in the Cloud of God's Mind for many thousands of years (in our understanding of time), when we are rebooted on the new earth, not a moment will have passed. Any other way requires some form of hardware for us to have any conscious existence. And what does this mean? Provisional heavenly bodies? Maybe we will float around on clouds playing harps. If so, I, for one, I suspect will be thinking eagerly of that new day when I get my faster processor and can get back to work.

Thinking about my memories being preserved in this way, plus all the data and all the programming that is being stored up in my already fading brain, has caused me to think about how I conduct my life a little differently. When I combine this with Polkinghorne's view that God has created a world that makes itself, the two provide a powerful incentive combined with an unexpected fear. If it is true, as it now increasingly seems to me, that God has given this entire world, including me, much more freedom to do with it as we please, it comes with an awesome responsibility. We are creatures, created beings, who have some control over who we become. I am to a large degree responsible for my experiences and memories. More than the data of my memories, I am also responsible for some of the programming. I am also responsible for everything that fills my brain except for the genetic information that I was provided with as part of my unique creation. That means every bit of data becomes important because it becomes part of those patterns that I will carry with me when I get my upgrade. Do I want really to have that anger that I hold against someone who has hurt me, do I want a gross and debasing image stuck in my brain? Do I want to hold a reprehensible thought or plot in that memory bank? Perhaps God has a way of sweeping the code and making it clean and in that there is hope. But if I am answerable for the condition and quality of the data as well as the programming within the unique hardware I have been given, it means I must exercise caution but also must look to joyfully fill it with everything that is right, and good and pure. It makes me who I am and who I will be, not just now, but in the new earth as well.

Chapter 7
Observation: Why Consciousness is Necessary

I think I first woke up when lying on my back watching the clouds. It might have been walking from the dimly lit barn on a moonless night toward the welcoming house and looking up to see the stars. It was on one of these occasions that I can vaguely recall thinking about God. It started my knees shaking. These were my own thoughts about God and distinctly not the same thoughts that were provided to me by a slightly bombastic preacher every Sunday. My father and mother, both Dutch and strongly in the Calvinist reformed tradition would never miss the half hour drive to church any more than they would miss pouring a cup of coffee heavy with cream and sugar for a drop-in guest. But the God this fresh, new consciousness was seeking seemed far removed from the neatly buttoned-down God that always seemed to be talked about in three tidy points.

Annie Dillard has written beautifully of the process of a child waking up, that is becoming conscious in the fully human sense we mean. In *An American Childhood* she recounts her own wakening in crystalline detail at about the age of 10:

"But, it was not an event as if coming into a room. It was much more like waking from a deep sleep on a lazy Saturday or Sunday morning when there are no pressing duties to attend to and in that blissful half sleep half awake mode you cannot come up with a single compelling reason why you should not just continue to enjoy this halfway land."

My awakening came in fits and starts, too, as I suspect yours did. There are two great mysteries that confound scientists today and they are the unlikely and completely non-intuitive nature of particle behavior at the quantum level, and the other is consciousness. How can we be certain there is such a thing as consciousness? I can be quite certain that I am conscious, but as for you, I am forced to take your word for it. It turns out that there is a pretty solid objective proof for consciousness, but to offer that I would have to take you deep into the mysteries of quantum mechanics and we're not quite ready to go there yet.

Consciousness is rather difficult to define. Augustine of Hippo said when asked to define time, that when he didn't think about it he knew what it was, but when asked to explain it, he found it almost impossible. That seems even more true of consciousness. The naturalist, quite naturally, believes that consciousness is an inevitable result of the increasing complexity of evolution. The philosopher Daniel Dennett, one of the most virulent anti-theists writing today, believes he has unraveled the mysteries of consciousness in his book *Consciousness Explained*. For him, and most likely most naturalists, the only possible explanation is to be found in ever-deeper study of the very complex processing and neural network functions of the "computer made of meat" that we carry above our necks.

Speaking of computers, Ray Kurzweil is a leader among those who believe, essentially based in the naturalist conviction of the evolution of complexity, that computers will have consciousness, if they cannot be said to have it already today. There is much discussion today about "the Singularity," that moment when artificial intelligence becomes superintelligence and therefore, conscious. Kurzweil thinks that will be about 2045. The amazing power of today's computers in processing very complex tasks is truly astounding, but nothing compared to what is coming with the development of massively complex parallel processors using quantum mechanical processes. But then animal brains are amazingly complex as well. How can a bird with a brain the size of a bean or a small pea know exactly where to find its home when a 3000 mile flight is called for? Indeed, some philosophers including the Christian philosopher Richard Swinburne consider that the higher forms of animals are indeed conscious.

I do not think it a coincidence that I equated my own sense of awakening with deep and sometimes troubling thoughts of God. I certainly do not think that essential in all cases, but the thoroughly natural human tendency to seek after God is one of the distinguishing characteristics of human consciousness. Anthropologists have concluded that Neandertals, not even homo sapiens, likely had thoughts of the afterlife based on their burial practices that included the implements the living thought the dead would need in the next life. In fact, if this searching after God and immortality is missing, we must ask why? It is clearly such an essential part of human experience it seems that a defining element of humanity is missing from someone who could truthfully say that the question of God, or ultimate origins, or ultimate purpose never occurred to them.

If searching for God is indeed one universal aspect of consciousness, it hardly seems possible to me that computers would develop this aspect entirely on their own. Of course, they could be programmed by humans to ask that question, but then it is not the computer or machines consciousness at work, is it? The machine is simply a tool of the searcher. And, as dearly as I may have loved my German wirehair pointer, and as intelligent as I sometimes considered her to be, I cannot think for a moment that she looked up at stars, wondered what was beyond them, and what her life really meant. I often laughed while she was sleeping. Her muffled barks and legs moving with herky jerky enthusiasm clearly demonstrated her dream life, which I am confident consisted mostly of wildly free chases after rabbits and ringneck pheasants. I never once saw in those sleep-filled behaviors the slightest evidence that she was in pursuit of the hound of heaven. But then, how do I know? I can't even be sure that you are conscious let alone my late dog.

Understanding consciousness has become one of the most critical searches in all of science, and now, I dare say, theology. If the quite firmly fixed belief of the naturalist about consciousness being an inevitable culmination of ever growing complexity of evolution, then, in many respects heaven will be torn from the skies and the idea of the spiritual and supernatural will be dealt a potential deathblow. In many respects the jump from inanimate molecules transforming into chemicals with the ability to process food, reproduce and evolve into higher form is considerably less than the jump from unconscious life into full blown consciousness. So consciousness and the necessity of explaining both how it came to be and why it is inevitable is a high challenge for the biologist and chemist. Consciousness also represents a deep challenge to physicists as we will shortly explore.

For the theologian, consciousness is an essential element of some of the most significant underlying structures of understanding our world and our place in it. If we can create machines with consciousness, if there is no distinct difference between our consciousness and that of a dolphin or whale, or cow even, then the Animal Liberation Front people are perfectly right in their horror of our choices in recreation and food. Their violence in protecting the lives of cows, pigs and probably slugs will round out to not just be justified, but an exercise in high morality as they claim. Then, when does pulling a plug on a machine become murder, as Kurzweil asks in *How to Create A Mind*?

Consciousness as uniquely human will increasingly come into play in Christian (as well as Jewish and Islamic) theological discussions as the evolution of the human species from lower forms of life becomes increasingly accepted as the truth. That transition from unconscious life to sentient being, whether it happened over eons or in an "Adam and Eve" moment seems to me essential to the Christian understanding of God and his special relationship to the creatures we call human. If that distinction is lost then I have a hard time seeing what sense we can make of the purpose of creation, free will, evil, sin, redemption and immortality.

Perhaps more to the point of this book, how can we pray without this distinction of consciousness as a uniquely human characteristic? If prayer is reducible to the mere passage of minute electrical impulses between the wet neurons in our brains then the likes of Dennett and other naturalists are fully justified in their self-righteous pity for us when we pray. We are indeed pathetically deluded.

As I write these words, clumsily, on my generation one iPad, I watch a bonneted baby play in the grassy lawn on which I lounge while enjoying a cheap cigar. The sounds of soft ocean waves blends with the excessive cheeriness of tropical birds and a soft breeze playing with the palm fronds above my head. I'm in Maui and the beauty of the piercing green of the condo lawn against the blue sky and turquoise water is sometimes more than I can bear. I want so much to capture it, hold it, absorb it, inhale it, let it become me and be part of me, not just for now and for memory sake. I want it to become part of me and this experience of peace and beauty to exist uninterrupted for all eternity. And I am aware of that experience, as I am aware of the fleeting nature of it. I am aware that it is I, a unique, one-of-a-kind human being who is experiencing this. Good luck to the artificial intelligence creators in thinking they can make machines that can experience, communicate and convince others that they are experiencing similar longings. Good luck to the naturalists who are intent on proving that the primordial muck was able to generate this kind of life all on its own.

Such experiences and the sharing of such experiences may or may not help to convince you that there is something very real and unique about consciousness. But, confront contemporary quantum mechanics, and you may think about consciousness and its possible role in how the universe works in a new and intriguing way.

Prayer, it seems, is not possible without consciousness. But, as some physicists see things, more than prayer is missing if consciousness is not present. In one way of looking at the physical world, the entire massive universe is not possible without consciousness. Let me repeat that. The physical world it appears is not possible without consciousness or mind to measure and experience it. At least, that appears to be one of the answers to the trouble puzzle of the "measurement problem" in current physics. The measurement problem is one of the greatest mysteries in contemporary physics. There is no firm answer to the problems posed by measurement, problems related to the connection between the microscopic quantum world and the world we experience in our daily lives known as the world of classical physics.

The suggestion of some is that for our world to exist, consciousness is required because, strangely, it seems to require a conscious mind to cause a particle "wave collapse" necessary to measure it. Measuring it changes it, and that means changes the world that the particle impacts. And measurement seems to require a mind. No doubt you are thinking I have gone too far with my mystical musings here. So I ask you to bear with me as we dig a little deeper into a topic that confounds most anyone involved in quantum mechanics. Remember, as you try and wrap your head around some of these ideas that Nobel laureate Richard Feynman said: "If you think you understand quantum mechanics, you don't understand quantum mechanics."

The deep understanding of our physical world at the smallest levels began with a search for a better understanding of light. Think about it. What is light? How do we see what we do? We know that what we see is largely made possible by the light from the sun? The moon is reflected light from the sun as are the planets, but the stars, they generate their own light. What is it? Our eyes capture it and our brain interprets what we see, but what is light made of?

Since light is all around us and such an essential part of our existence, inquiring scientific minds have been trying to come to grips with its nature since, well, almost the beginning. In 300 BC the Greek philosopher and mathematician Euclid wrote Optica, which said that light traveled in straight lines and questioned the earlier belief that light originated in the eye as a beam. The idea of light as a wave was first published in the 1660s by Robert Hooke and expanded by Christiaan Huygens in 1678. The wave theory said that light traveled from its source like a wave on a body of water or a sound wave. This theory worked pretty well in that light waves were subject to interference just like water and sound waves. That's because waves have wavelengths which are the distance between the peak of the wave and the trough. When two waves meet, they interfere with each other so that if both waves meet at the peak then the one wave that comes out of it is doubled in size. But, if the peak of one wave meets up with the trough of another, then the wave is cancelled out and it disappears. This aspect of waves is important as we go forward to look at what we know of the physical universe.

Waves could be measured in both how fast they traveled and by their wavelength which was called frequency. The frequency of the wavelengths are observed by us as different colors of light which can be separated out by using a prism. We see colors in the rainbow as the water droplets serve as many prisms, breaking the light into its various frequencies. It was understood that for waves to have an existence they needed something to move in. For waves in the ocean it was water, for sound it was air. But light traveled even in a vacuum so it didn't need air and clearly water wasn't needed. So the scientists said that the medium through which light travels must permeate the entire universe and they called it the "luminiferous ether."

Isaac Newton didn't think this wave theory held water, so to speak. He said in his 1675 work Hypothesis of Light that light was made up of corpuscles or particles of matter. This left some scientific thinkers thinking light was a wave and some that it was a particle. In 1845 Michael Faraday found that light was related to electromagnetism, that strange force that pulled magnets together or pushed them apart. Electromagnetic waves didn't need a medium to operate in so the ether, a theory never verified by experiment or experience, wasn't needed. A big breakthrough came when James Clerk Maxwell in 1873 published his mathematical equations which clearly demonstrated that light was a form of electromagnetic radiation. These famous equations were then experimentally verified by Heinrich Hertz who created radio waves in his laboratory. To this day, we measure the wavelengths of radio waves and light in hertz. So the waves of electromagnetism by which (until cable and now the Internet) we used to get our radio and TV signals, are the same as light except of a different frequency measured in hertz. Maxwell's elegant equation also said that light would travel at a constant speed which already had been measured, granting further substance to this important equation. The speed of light was determined to be the speed limit of the universe. Nothing could move faster than 186,000 miles per second. That's pretty fast, but not fast enough as we now know.

This was the state of scientific understanding of light as we moved into the 20th century. Isaac Newton, it seemed, was proven wrong and the scientific community found Maxwell's equations, proven by experiment, to be beyond question. It was this sort of thing that was bringing such confidence to the scientific community and beyond in the ability of science to describe our world: a brilliant mind coming up with a very elegant, even beautiful, mathematical equation which then was fully and completely verified by experience.

In 1894 a young German physicist by the name of Max Planck was hired by electric companies to help them create maximum light from light bulbs with minimum energy. He studied a big problem at that time called "black body radiation," and determined that light or any electromechanical energy could only be emitted in discrete quantities, called "quanta." This idea was pretty well dismissed by the scientific community because of its apparent contradiction with Maxwell's beautiful equation. But, in 1905 a rogue physicist working in a lowly clerk's job in a patent office in Switzerland because he couldn't get even a high school physics teaching job, published four groundbreaking papers including one on the photoelectric effect. The paper used Planck's analysis of quanta to demonstrate how electrons were thrown off from matter when hit by electromagnetic radiation.

The young physicist was Albert Einstein. What Einstein demonstrated is what is now called the wave-particle duality and it was the start of the understanding of our physical world now called quantum mechanics. Einstein's paper, *On a Heuristic Viewpoint Concerning the Production and Transformation of Light*, showed that energy in the form of light existed in discrete packets as Planck had suggested. This made light operate like particles rather than waves. Einstein called those packets of energy photons. So, it looked like Newton's idea of "corpuscles" of energy was right after all. The problem was that Maxwell's equation exactly predicted how light would behave and that was as a wave. By now, numerous experiments had proven that light was a wave. So if Einstein was right, light was a wave and a particle.

We talked about this earlier, but here is where science really starts to conflict with common sense, intuition and how we experience life and the physical world. Waves are waves, particles are particles. Bullets or stones don't have much in common with what we see in the ocean, lake or our bathtub. Yet, here the greatest scientific thinkers in the world are saying, well, actually, light is both a wave and particle. What is even stranger, they went on to see that not just light is that way, but the entire physical world at its deepest level shares this fundamental contradiction. Prince Louis de Broglie demonstrated that all particles, not just light particles, also had wave properties.

Once this basic contradiction became more widely accepted as an accurate description of what was going on, things started to move relatively quickly in this new world of particle physics. And things got stranger, and stranger and stranger. Werner Heisenberg, a young German physicist, came up with what is now known as the Heisenberg Uncertainty Principle which we discussed earlier. These strange things called particles were very hard to pin down. In fact, Heisenberg showed mathematically, if you pinned down their location, you could not know how fast they were going. And if you could measure how fast they were going, you pretty much lost sight of their position. This contradicts our experience and so we tend to reject it. We can use a variety of means to measure exactly where a car is at in a moment of time, and at the same time we can know how fast it is going. Not so with the elements that make up that car.

Now, I must add a word of caution to anything I say about this critically important principle and I will use the words of one of the best teachers of science to the public today, Brian Cox: "Heisenberg's Uncertainty Principle is one of the most misunderstood parts of quantum theory, a doorway through which all sorts of charlatans and purveyors of tripe can force their philosophical musings." Brian is British so to translate, the equivalent of "tripe" might be two letters in American common usage: "B.S." And I'm quite certain that Mr. Cox would consider most of my musings here to be the kind of tripe he refers to. So, to be safe from Mr. Cox's thunder, I'll quote him directly about this principle:

"In other words, if we start out by confining a particle to be in a smaller and smaller region, then it has a tendency to want to jump further and further away from that region. This is so important it is worth restating a third time: the more precisely you know the position of a particle at some instant, the less well you know how fast it is moving and therefore where it will be sometime later. This is exactly Heisenberg's statement of the Uncertainty Principle. It lies at the heart of quantum theory."

You are wondering what all this has to do with consciousness and its role in bringing the physical world into being. We are getting closer to that so hang in there with me just a bit longer. What Cox, through Heisenberg, is saying is that a particle moves around a lot. In fact, it can move throughout the entire Universe. That's because, remember, its not really a particle but a wave and a wave can be pretty spread out. Apparently all particles jump around pretty quickly and far because Cox says, "Indeed, its (Uncertainty Principle) origin lies in our proposition that a particle can be anywhere in the Universe an instant after we measure its position." Hold on, you can't measure the position of a wave that is spread out all over the place, but since a particle is, well, a particle, you can pin it down to some location. But then you can't know how fast it is going and you can't know if in the very next instant after you nailed down its position it won't be on the other side of a galaxy a billion light years away.

This is all strange indeed. But it deals with particles at the very smallest levels and so we seem safe from some of these strange goings on. Things don't happen this way at our human scale, let alone the scale of galaxies. But all things including the entire physical universe are made up of just a few different types of particles with strange names like quarks and bosons and leptons and gluons and the like. So, at some level, what happens deep inside atoms also affects the world we live in. If a grain of sand, small to us, but monstrous at the sub-atomic particle level behaved as the particles which make it up did, we could see it, note its position and the next instant it could be out beyond Betelgeuse. But it doesn't happen like that to particles at this size. The mathematics (and our experience with grains of sand) shows that it doesn't because of a time element. But, the grain of sand still follows quantum laws and it still actually moves. Cox: "Although we discovered that the particle will most likely not remain at rest, we also discovered that for large objects – and a grain of sand is very large indeed in quantum terms – this motion is completely undetectable."

Let's go back to what Brian Cox said. He said a particle could be anywhere in the Universe the instant we measure its position. Measuring particles is the key to what we are talking about here. Because here a deep mystery unfolds. Physicists call this the "measurement problem" and a great many of the brainiest in the world are trying to understand this better and its implications. It is an enigma, a quantum enigma, as some have called it. We have pictured atoms as a nucleus with an electron spinning around it. There's the proton and neutron all stuck together in the middle and the electron spinning around this nucleus furiously. But, since the electron is a particle and we now know that particles are both waves and particles we can't really picture it as a neat little ball anymore. The electron operates in a cloud. The electron doesn't spin around hidden in the cloud, the electron is the cloud. But when we go look for where this electron is exactly, when we identify its position, something strange happens. Instead of the cloud, we see a particle. This is called a "collapse."

The trick is that whenever we measure the position of the particle, the range of locations narrows just enough so that we never see the wave, a process called wave collapse. The reason we know the wave exists is because it determines the possible range over which we might see the particle. If this seems far fetched to you, you're in good company: what exactly happens when a particle-wave collapses is still debated by physicists today. In fact, here's the Wikipedia definition: "the measurement problem in quantum mechanics is the unresolved problem of how (or *whether*) wavefunction collapse occurs." So, if we aren't even certain if a wavefunction collapse occurs, let's put that part of it off for a bit.

While there seems to be much debate in scientific circles about this collapse and what it really means, one thing seems certain: observing particles and measuring them does something of fundamental importance. The particle operates as a wave with indeterminate and indeterminable location and speed. But, when we observe it or measure it, the wave collapses and we can measure either (but not both) speed or location. This raises the issue of the tree falling in the forest. If no one is there to hear it fall, does it make a sound? Here we are asking, if no one observes a particle, does it have a physical reality? Prior to the collapse, a particle is cloud of infinite possibilities. It could be here, it could be a zillion miles away. Once observed, the possibilities disappear until it is released from observation and collapse and returns to what is called its "superposition state."

Since we know that all of the created world is made up of these particles that behave in this way, what does this mean for the world we experience everyday? As we have seen, while there absolutely is a seamless connection, understanding the jumps between the micro and macro worlds is still very mysterious. But we know the observer or measurement makes a difference, a huge difference, at the particle level so at some point there is an inevitable connection to our world of everyday experience.

Let's take a little closer look at what we mean by observing. Does it matter who the observer is? Does the tree make a sound? Scientists define a sound as vibration transmitted to the senses interpreted by our brains. So, while vibration in the air occurs it is just vibration until it is heard by something with ears and a brain. That doesn't mean a human, of course. A bird could hear it, or a deer. Here's where things get really interesting. Does a wave collapse if a bird observes it? Or a deer? It turns out that the answer is, as far as can be seen right now, no. Unless the bird or deer, or computer, is conscious. Remarkably, mysteriously collapsing the wave requires a conscious mind.

The simple but incredibly profound fact that current science has uncovered is that our physical world as described by quantum mechanics cannot exist without consciousness--at least that is what some brave souls in physics suggest. Euan Squires, a distinguished physicist from England, author of *Conscious Mind in the Physical World*, said, "Every interpretation of quantum mechanics involves consciousness." Nobel laureate in physics, Eugene Wigner stated: "When the province of physical theory was extended to encompass microscopic phenomena through the creation of quantum mechanics, the concept of consciousness came to the fore again. It was not possible to formulate the laws of quantum mechanics in a fully consistent way without reference to the consciousness." Or, one of our most respected scientists, Freeman Dyson: "It would not be surprising if it should turn out that the origin and destiny of the energy in the universe cannot be completely understood in isolation from the phenomena of life and consciousness...It is conceivable...that life may have a larger role to play than we have imagined."

Or not. That's the problem. Most physicists today apparently resist the suggestion that Dyson so carefully makes. Understandable. It suggests that the world is brought into being by consciousness. As Professor Bradley, math professor emeritus of Calvin College pointed out to me in personal correspondence: "The idea that 'collapsing the wave requires a conscious mind' is regarded as a fringe idea. Bohr introduced it in the earliest days of quantum mechanics and a few lesser figures afterwards picked up on it. But it never became mainstream. Here's a thought experiment that may help. The universe is 13.7 billion years old, our earth around 4 billion years. Homo sapiens have been on earth roughly 400,000 years. Scientists who observe quantum phenomena have been around roughly 100 years. Do you really want to say that quantum collapse never occurred before 100 years ago? And if you do, how important is quantum collapse – it certainly hasn't shaped the world in any significant way. Or do you want to say that God is the consciousness present at every collapse. But God sees all particles all the time. So how could any wave collapse? Wouldn't it always be collapsed?"

Herein lies the dilemma and enigma. The history of our world in classical physics makes it clear that life arrived on the scene billions of years after particles and laws first burst forth from that singularity at the big bang. But quantum physics suggests that the somehow life, mind, consciousness may have something to do with the world as it was is and will be.

But what is it that makes conscious life so special that it can have this kind of real affect on particles, energy and the creation of our world? Can't machines also measure? Why is consciousness required? It is well established that no machine can observe or measure the particle to cause its collapse unless a conscious mind is involved. Machines are obviously used to measure particle activity, such as Geiger counters that famously click when encountering radioactivity. But *Quantum Enigma* authors make it clear that a machine alone cannot cause the collapse: "In his rigorous 1932 treatment, *The Mathematical Foundations of Quantum Mechanics*, John von Neumann showed that quantum theory makes physics encounter with consciousness inevitable." The authors explained how von Neumann showed that the Geiger counter shares the superposition, or quantum state of the particle and therefore would be simultaneously in a "fired and unfired state" until there was a conscious mind to take note of it. What about if they rigged up another machine to watch and register if the Geiger counter clicked?

"Should a second isolated measuring apparatus come into contact with the Geiger counter – for example, an electronic recording device recording whether the Geiger counter has fired – it joins the superposition state and records both situations existing simultaneously. This so-called 'von Neumann chain' can continue indefinitely... However, when we look at the Geiger counter, we will always see a particular result, not a superposition. Von Neumann concluded that only a conscious observer can actually make an observation."

Quantum Enigma authors Rosenblum and Kuttner argue this discovery of science dating back to 1932 is the only objective proof that consciousness actually exists. If these physicists are correct (and I find their arguments quite compelling) then science has proven the necessity and certainly the existence of consciousness. But, this whole idea does not sit well with a great many in the science community who are very uneasy with the potential metaphysical or even spiritual consequences of this fact. As the authors say in the first chapter, "This is a controversial book. But nothing we say about quantum mechanics is controversial. The experimental results we report and our explanation of them with quantum theory are completely undisputed. It is the **mystery** these results imply beyond physics that is hotly disputed [their emphasis]. For many physicists, this mystery, the quantum enigma, is best not talked about. It displays physics' encounter with consciousness. It's the skeleton in our closet."

Because of this extreme discomfort many great minds have been working on interpretations of the clearly established facts that would do away with the mystery. Rosenblum and Kuttner walk through ten currently contending interpretations. Essentially all of them wind up with consciousness as a requirement.

The measurement problem has spawned all kinds of intriguing thoughts and ideas. One of the first to highlight the rather extreme problems caused by this discovery was Erwin Schrödinger's. Despite all his contributions, it seems when his name comes up it is in reference to his cat. "Schrödinger's Cat" was posed as a thought experiment to highlight the problems associated with measurement and the wavefunction collapse. Let me quote Wikipedia on this:

The best known example is the "paradox" of the Schrödinger's cat. A mechanism is arranged to kill a cat if a quantum event, such as the decay of a radioactive atom, occurs. Thus the fate of a large scale object, the cat, is entangled with the fate of a quantum object, the atom. Prior to observation, according to the Schrodinger equation, the cat is apparently evolving into a linear combination of states that can be characterized as an "alive cat" and states that can be characterized as a "dead cat". Each of these possibilities is associated with a specific nonzero probability amplitude; the cat seems to be in some kind of "combination" state called a "quantum superposition". However, a single, particular observation of the cat does not measure the probabilities: it always finds either a living cat, or a dead cat. After the measurement the cat is definitively alive or dead. The question is: How are the probabilities converted into an actual, sharply well-defined outcome?"

Then there is the "many worlds" explanation first suggested by Hugh Everett. In this idea there is no actual wavefunction collapse, which means that since the particle/wave can be anywhere, any time with a multitude of histories and futures, there must be many worlds that exist simultaneously. There is one world where the particle is here, another there and so on. "Many" doesn't even begin to describe just how many worlds there must be for this explanation to work. Yet, it is one of the leading ideas to explain this measurement/collapse problem.

Rosenblum and Kuttner conclude: "'Many worlds may be the most bizarre description of reality ever proposed." That certainly seems true, and it looks to an amateur observer such as myself that these are extreme directions to take to avoid uncomfortable conclusions. But that may be unfair. Whatever the answer to the wavefunction collapse enigma may turn out to be, it seems certain to seem both strange and metaphysical. And that makes many in the science world very uncomfortable.

A hint of that may be seen in the many books addressing concerns about unproven, unprovable and metaphysical speculations. An example is Jim Baggott's 2013 book *Farewell to Reality: How Modern Physics Has Betrayed the Search for Scientific Truth*. Referring to Feynman's quote that no one understands quantum mechanics, Baggott says:

"Some modern theoretical physicists have sought to compensate for this loss of understanding. Others have tried to paper over the cracks in theories that are clearly not up to the task. Or they have pushed, with vaulting ambition, for 'a theory of everything.' These physicists have been led -- unwittingly or otherwise -- into myth creation and fairy tales."

The ideas, such as "many worlds," proposed to deal with the measurement/observation problem do often sound like fairy tales. On the other hand, to many the idea of a conscious mind -- God or humans -- needed to bring the world into existence also sounds like a fairy tale.

George Berkeley, an Irish Bishop and philosopher, in the early 1700s promoted an idea he later called "subjective idealism." This idea said there was no reality to the physical world, instead familiar objects like tables and chairs only exist in our minds as we perceive them. This idea resulted in a limerick worth repeating (Quad refers to the central court area of a university):

There was a young fellow named Todd
Who said, "It's exceedingly odd
To think that this tree
Should continue to be
When there's no one about in the Quad.

This philosophical idea, three hundred years old, seems remarkably prescient. And the rejoinder limerick summarizes better than I could hope to just what that the implications of all this may be:

There's nothing especially odd;
I'm always about in the Quad.
And that's why this tree
Can continue to be
When observed by
Yours faithfully, God.

If I told you at the beginning of this chapter that the world cannot exist without conscious minds to see it, you may have shut the book or tablet computer thinking me a kook. If I told you that science tells us today that it is observation by a conscious mind that brings our physical world into a state where we can experience it, you'd think I was making things up. But Martin Rees is no kook or oddball. Martin Rees, Lord Rees of Ludlow, is UK's Royal Astronomer and was President of the Royal Society from 2005 to 2010. He is certainly one of the most well-known and respected scientists. Here is what Lord Rees said on this mystery:

"In the beginning there were only probabilities. The universe could only come into existence if someone observed it. It does not matter that the observers turned up several billions years later on. The universe exists because we are aware of it."

Regardless of what is ultimately found to solve the measurement problem, assuming something is, the important thing to understand is that it will have profound implications for our understanding of the world, and just possibly our understanding of God and our place in it.

Chapter 8
Authority: Who Owns the Truth

"Jesus loves me this I know, for the Bible tells me so."

Those words and that little song were among the first words I ever learned, among the first words and song my children learned, and now among the first words my grandchildren are learning.

If you are one like me who grew up in an environment where that song was taught so early, you can appreciate the anguish of those in that community when something comes along to threaten their confidence in the Bible as God's inerrant word. For those who did not grow up in such a world, I can only try to help you understand that anguish by analogy. Did you believe that Santa Claus was real? And how did you feel when you were forced to confront the facts? That's a very weak analogy. Have you been in a happy, trusting, intimate relationship only to shockingly discover that you have been horribly and forever betrayed? That comes closer to the anguish. When suddenly everything that you have based your life on turns out to be false, you are inevitably rocked to your very foundations.

The entire hope and faith of most of the two-plus billion Christians in the world are completely tied to the belief that a lowly carpenter from a small Jewish village more than 2000 years ago was actually God in flesh, was horribly tortured to death and then walked out of his grave on his own power and, in full sight of his followers, rose up into the clouds with the promise that he would return and bring his followers into a life without end meant for them. Believers with strong confidence in that story willingly sacrifice their lives, their livelihoods, all that they have and are, based on that belief. The confidence of that belief is tied very much to their confidence in the absolute truth of the words written in the years following Jesus' death and rising all the way back to the earliest recordings of the special relationship between the One true God and his chosen people, the Israelites.

The relationship of Christian believers to the Bible highlights the important issue of authority. The question of authority is among the most important of our lives. And, particularly so when talking about prayer and what we can know about it.

Whom do you trust to tell you the truth?
Whom do you believe?
How do you know where true authority lies?
How do you know what you believe or think you know is the truth?

We're not just talking about prayer here. Whom do you trust to tell you what food is safe to eat or what repairman to trust with your car? In what or in whom do you place confidence to tell you the truth about the nature of this world, why the stars don't fall on our heads, or why things exist as oppose to not existing? As you think about those questions, the direction that you are inclined to take will tell more about where you stand on matters of faith and belief than almost anything. If you say the Bible, then you stand in the tradition dating not just back to the mid-300s when the New Testament canon was pretty well established, you go back to the Hebrew scriptures or Torah which date back to the time of Moses or at least King Josiah (640 BCE). If you say science, you stand with perhaps the majority of those in the Western World and beyond, who have come to trust what scientists teach as the most reliable guide to what is real and true.

What about those, like me, who stand in both streams? In light of what science teaches, can we treat the Bible, both Old and New Testaments, as the authoritative, inerrant, divinely inspired revelation of God? Because of its apparent contradictions with science, do we toss it out entirely as a sham, do we selectively accept the parts that don't contradict, or do we look to reinterpret it hoping that by doing so we can do away with most if not all contradictions?

Our answer to this question of authority will determine to a great degree our entire belief system and therefore how we deal with our daily experiences of life—including our thoughts about the future and eternity. As I survey the landscape of Christian belief today, I see all kinds of different responses to this challenge. Here are some approaches being taken:

1.   Firm adherence to literal inerrancy.
2.   Rejection of biblical authority in favor of internal guidance.
3.   Selective acceptance.
4.   Reinterpretation including restating inerrancy.
5.   Concordism—reinterpreting to eliminate apparent contradictions.
6.   Head in the sand.

While some fit firmly into one or other category, I suspect that many, like me, could be found at various times in almost any of these categories.

1. Firm adherence to literal inerrancy

This is the most conservative and fundamentalist of positions on biblical authority. At its most extreme it becomes cultish or fully separated from the mainstream of society. For example, there was a preacher a number of years ago who taught that every man must wear a crew cut because of some text he found that referred to men needing short hair. Others teach that women must be silent in church because there is a passage in the Bible that gives that instruction. Others teach that the earth is flat because the Bible refers to its "four corners." Even Biblical literalists today tend to think such extreme positions are out of line.

The frontline of this question of authority today tends to be the confrontation with science: the Bible says God created the universe in six days and therefore it was six days. The genealogy of the Bible tracing to Adam and Eve only goes back about 6000 years and therefore that is how old the universe is. This was taught by Irish Bishop Ussher and it represents a line in the sand for many devout believers. There are "young earth creationists" who study the world to find validation for the 6000 year age of the universe. This position was given a tremendous boost in 1960 with the publication of *The Genesis Flood* by Henry Morris and John Whitcomb, who provided geologic evidence for a world that was formed largely by the biblical flood.

But this position on authority has a great problem: it is in direct contradiction to what we know of the universe through science. The age of the universe appears to be very well established—about 13.7 billion years old. So, if you believe it to be 6000 years old, you either choose to completely ignore the facts and evidence or you believe that God created the universe 6000 years ago with the appearance of a much greater age. The same goes with the creation of life. Science teaches that life with all its diversity evolved through natural processes. Leaving aside the difficult and unresolved issues of the origin of life and whether or not evolution was guided or unguided by an intelligent designer, evolution itself is not controversial from the science perspective. It is established fact in its foundational propositions. However, that contradicts the creation of life as presented in Genesis with a literal reading. God scooped up the dust of the earth to create Adam, the first human and male, and created Eve, the first female, from one of Adam's ribs. We cannot, in the literalist view, both have evolved from one-celled organisms and appeared as living, breathing humans in one moment of time. So one must choose, and to choose science as the authority in this contradiction for many is the rejection of the entire basis of their faith. If the Bible cannot be trusted in telling us how the universe and life began, how can it be trusted when it tells us how to live and die, and how to attain eternal glory? The stakes are very high which results in great fear, anger, and a willingness to do almost anything to protect what one has bet their whole lives on.

2. Rejection of biblical authority in favor of internal guidance.

This view does not mean that the Bible is rejected. It just means that the Bible, along with science, is deemed secondary on the issue of authority compared to intuition, spiritual contemplation and what feels right. We usually make decisions to some degree at least on what feels right to us. How do you know who to choose to spend your life with? How do you decide which car is right for you, or which home, or which community to live in, or which job to take? Certainly there is a thinking, intellectual element to many of these decisions and some rely more on head than heart and vice versa. But this just takes this normal decision-making about life decisions and applies it to this question of authority. How do I know what is right and wrong? I'll trust my gut. How do I determine fact from fiction? My instinct.

I sense that this view is much more widely adopted than most realize. It is in synch with some important cultural changes that we have witnessed and are very much involved in. Those include the high value of pluralism and its related philosophical and epistemological shift called "post-modernism." Without getting too philosophical here, these are connected based on the now widespread cultural ideal of equality in value, thought and personhood, which I'm calling pluralism. This is really quite a remarkable thing that has evolved. We don't see it as remarkable because we are in the soup, so to speak, and it is hard to step out of it to observe what is happening.

Pluralism is a reaction against something, as most movements are. We have seen the devastation of our world caused by separation, the creation of "we vs. them," of religion and politics-inspired violence, of racism, of discrimination. We reject the "inclusivism" that drives much of this and strive to become far more accepting of those of different colors, different beliefs, different values, different sexual orientations, and different nations. We accept things that we might otherwise have rejected and found intolerable because tolerance is nearly the highest value of all. In fact, the one thing those who value tolerance find intolerable is intolerance. The current debate of over gay rights is one of the front lines in this battle for pluralism. To reject homosexuality is intolerant and in the name of toleration, intolerant, "hateful" and discriminatory views must be firmly rejected by legislation, by social pressure and by force if necessary.

Pluralism can be seen as a deeply Christian value. Acceptance of others and rejection of the hatred and violence so embedded in religious belief are very positive changes and can be seen as wholly consistent with the teachings of Jesus, a God of love and the coming Kingdom of rule by God. But then we have these social value conflicts such as abortion, stem cell research, gay rights including gay marriage and with these come an apparent direct conflict with Biblical teaching and Biblical authority.

Pluralism and post-modernism can be seen as linked in relation to truth and authority. We need to accept and have dialog with people and groups holding different faiths, but we are told we can only really do so if we put aside the inclination to evangelize and proselytize. In post-modernist language, we deconstruct those beliefs and ideas that got us here. We're led to reject the meta-narratives that have driven our ideas, values and personal lives. We're to accept that truth is personal: what is true for you is true for you and what is true for me is true for me. In this post-modern, pluralistic value system there can be great acceptance: If I say I am a Christian because I believe in God and Jesus as the Son of God, good for me, for me that is truth. You are a Muslim because you believe in Allah and the teachings of Mohammed. Good for you, that is truth for you and now we can both get along just fine. You are gay, I am straight (or vice versa), good for both of us. I am black, you are white or Hispanic or Asian or whatever. Good for us. Putting aside our different ideas and beliefs depends on, in this view, accepting that there is no universal truth (except perhaps pluralism and tolerance) and that there is no need or value in trying to determine if one's "truth" is better than the other's "truth."

This gets applied to the issue of Biblical authority because it is both comfortable in the cultural soup we find ourselves in, and it conforms to something deep inside us, which is confidence in our own internal ability to sort out truth from falsehood. We don't normally walk around with the full knowledge and acceptance that what we believe in is false. We believe what we believe because we believe it to be true. Belief determines action: if I believe that field out there may be full of mines or improvised explosive devices, I'm probably not going to walk out there. So we look at the passages of scripture where there appear to be conflicts with science, but also with cultural values such as gay rights, and we determine what is right for ourselves without directly throwing out the idea of biblical authority or inerrancy. If there are passages that make us uncomfortable and appear to violate our internal sense of right and wrong, we put them aside for later consideration or decide we simply don't understand and interpret them correctly. There is a close correlation here to the "head in the sand" approach, but this is more reassuring because of our confidence in being able to determine and commit to truth, however personal it may be.

There is only one significant problem with this approach: it is not orthodox, at least in the Reformation sense of scripture as the highest authority. In the orthodox understanding, the words of the Bible are the highest authority. In this post-modern view, our own internal guidance is used to determine what of the Bible we accept as authoritative or not. In this case, scripture, or more specifically, our interpretation of the Bible is determined by our internal guidance.

3. Selective acceptance

This is also closely aligned with the above approach. But it is more specific about what is accepted and rejected. We all do this. There are about 3000 members of the Flat Earth Society, which means that about 99.9999% of believers have rejected the literalist interpretation of Numbers 15:38, Ezekiel 7:2, Isaiah

11:12 and Job 37:3 and 38:13. We have chosen not to interpret those passages literally. This is a process that is going on with increasing frequency with passages that are considered to be in direct conflict with science. The six days of creation are seen as a translation issue and actually refer to six epochs or phases. The creation of Adam is seen by some as a culturally-related myth and not intended to be treated as a literal description of how God created humans.

We do that not just to challenging texts involving science, but also those involving culture and values. Take this passage from Corinthians:

"Let your women keep silence in the churches; for it is not permitted unto them to speak; but they are commanded to be under obedience, as also saith the law. And if they will learn any thing, let them ask their husbands at home: for it is a shame for women to speak in the church." (KJV)

There are some who follow these admonitions to the letter. But again, they are considered cultish, out of the mainstream, out of touch. To be in touch means selective acceptance and rejection and this very direct instruction is rejected.

Everyone who accepts the Bible's authority and views it as the inerrant Word of God has deep trouble with this idea of acceptance and rejection, even though they do it. The rejection is justified on different reasons: misinterpretation, the passage reflects the personal opinion of the biblical author rather than the authoritative Word of God, or the belief that the Bible necessarily must adopt changing cultural values to at least some degree. But we come to those conclusions with some degree of fear and trembling knowing that we risk throwing out the baby with the bath water. The fear behind it all is what one old Dutch elder in my church said when I, as leader of the youth group, requested that we have a youth service in church in which we would use guitars. He asked in his Dutch accent: "Yah, but vhat vill dis lead to?" Indeed, what will it lead to? It's a slippery slope. Once we accept the idea that we can accept or reject at will, what happens to the idea of inerrancy and biblical authority? Have we moved into pluralism and post-modernism as described above? There be dragons there.

4. Reinterpretation including restating inerrancy

In its simplest form inerrancy is the idea that God wrote the words found in the Bible and his message is contained in those words as they are commonly understood. Since God is without error and since he controlled every word written, those words are without error—inerrant. As an example, in Genesis 9 God gives the rainbow as a token of the covenant between humans and God that no more would a flood come to destroy all flesh: "And God said, This is the token of the covenant which I make between me and you and every living creature that is with you, for perpetual generations: I do set my bow in the cloud, and it shall be for a token of a covenant between me and the earth." (vs. 12-13, KJV) Those words are clear: God created the rainbow as a promise to not destroy the world again with a flood. That means, there was no rainbow until the time of Noah. That means for virtually all the 4.5 billion years of the earth's existence, there were no rainbows, which means that the physical process of refracting light into multiple colors through the prisms of the water droplets didn't exist until after the flood.

There are, of course, numerous examples like this, including the flat earth mentioned earlier. The doctrine of inerrancy is challenged every time there is a direct contradiction between the words of the Bible and facts as we know them. For those committed to inerrancy, there are several possible answers to this challenge. We can decide there were translation errors, that is, the original words inspired by God are correct but translation errors crept in. The most common response is to decide that we are simply not interpreting the words correctly. For example, the references to the four corners of the earth don't mean that God was wrong in his understanding of the nature of the earth he created, but that he allowed the writers to use a common literary reference that the readers would understand to mean "the entire earth." When we find geologic evidence for a vast regional flood in Mesopotamia, it is relatively easy to conclude the "world flood" that is told in Genesis does not mean that it covered the entire globe, but it covered the entire world known by the writer.

The battle over inerrancy and what it really means has waged back and forth in Christian circles over the years. In 1978, Christianity Today editor Harold Lindsell published an explosive book called *The Battle for the Bible*. He laid a firm line in the sand. You were not a true Christian, he taught, unless you subscribed to the dictation concept of the inspiration of the Bible and accepted that everything the Bible taught about science and history was literally true. That battle continues today as evidenced by the 2008 book by Gregory Beale, a professor at Westminster Theological Seminary and former president of the Evangelical Theological Society. The Amazon book description for *The Erosion of Inerrancy in Evangelicalism: Responding to New Challenges to Biblical Authority*, includes this summary:

"How can the Bible be historically inaccurate while still serving as the authoritative word on morality and salvation? Beale concludes that it cannot, and his work will aid all who support biblical inerrancy in defending their position against postmodern attacks. This is an issue that affects the entire body of Christ."

But such positions are increasingly hard to square with the ever-expanding body of knowledge in both science and history that contradict the plain meaning of the biblical words. As examples from ancient history, there is no reliable archaeological evidence to date for the Exodus, only a few intriguing hints. And the story of the Hebrews conquering Canaan in a series of decisive battles as told in Joshua and Judges is now seen as a far more complex, lengthy and nuanced change from Canaanite culture to Israelite culture. The history as contained in the Bible is not directly contradicted, but neither does it tell an accurate or complete story. The examples of contradiction are clearer in the realm of science. We have widely accepted evidence for the creation of the universe 13.7 billion years ago, not 6000 years ago as Biblical genealogy would suggest. We don't have a concept of a firmament so prominent in the Old Testament: a hard ceiling of sorts that holds back the waters released in the flood.

But many consider evolution the most challenging to the Biblical story. In scientific and academic circles the debate is no longer about whether evolution describes the development of life in its many forms, but whether or not the scientific evidence provides proof or inclination toward a directed evolution or undirected. Can we see in evolution evidence for God at work, or was the process started and then left to run on its own? But evolution itself is no longer seriously in question—except by those who are more or less in the Lindsell camp on inerrancy.

Clinging to inerrancy while contending with contradictory facts leads most to conclude that it is a matter of interpretation and understanding. In other words, the Biblical words are not "wrong," but merely misunderstood. The whole "young earth" controversy hangs on this reinterpretation strategy. Genesis isn't wrong when it says God created the world in six days, which directly contradicts scientific evidence of a much slower process, but we misinterpret "days" which can be understood be periods of time—very long periods of time. An intriguing reinterpretation of the Genesis 1 comes from John H. Walton of Wheaton College, who concludes in his book *The Lost World of Genesis One*, that we misunderstand the creation story entirely. It is not an account of the material creation of the universe, but a thoroughly culturally-bound account of the functional creation of the universe and the establishment of the cosmos as the temple of God.

While these are efforts to hold fast to inerrancy while dealing with the contradictory facts of science and history, the real reinterpretation is inerrancy itself. Most thinking believers would reject Lindsell's "dictation" approach. Most do not see inspiration in this direct form. While holding on to the idea of God intimately involved in the writing and message of the Bible, they can accept that the writers were not always writing with the advantage of divine omniscience, or perfect knowledge. Rarely did they escape their own limitations of culture, scientific understanding or misconceptions of history. But these "errors" do not necessarily make the Bible a book of errors. Inerrancy in this view applies to the theological, moral and spiritual messages of the Bible. The Evangelical Covenant church that I was a member of for many years talked about biblical inerrancy in terms of perfection in teaching on faith and life. That is hard to argue with and leaves plenty of room for acceptance of factual contradictions in matters of science, history and other established truths. But it remains a slippery ground on which to walk for those fearful of going too far from the dictation model of inspiration.

5. Concordism

I include "concordism" in this discussion not because it offers a different approach, but because the current debate about biblical authority and inerrancy often includes a discussion of this approach. Concordism refers to the belief that the Bible and science are not in conflict but in concord. The apparent differences and conflicts are resolved by various approaches of questioning the science or questioning the interpretations of scripture. Dr. Hugh Ross is the founder of Reasons to Believe, a ministry organization dedicated to directly addressing the issues of faith and science to bolster the faith of believers and challenge those who use science as a basis for rejecting the Christian faith. He is a leading proponent of concordism which is defined as "the belief that the book of nature and the book of Scripture significantly overlap and can be constructively integrated." Dr. Ross makes a distinction between what he calls "hard concordism" and "soft concordism:"

"Hard concordists look to make most, but not all, discoveries, new and old, in science agree with some passage of Scripture. Soft concordists seek agreement between properly interpreted

Scripture passages that describe some aspect of the natural realm and indisputably and well-established data in science. RTB [Reasons to Believe] holds the latter view."

There are all kinds of caveats in that carefully constructed definition, specifically "properly interpreted Scripture" and "indisputably and well established data in science." The debate, pointedly between John Walton of Wheaton College and Hugh Ross of Reasons to Believe, highlights a key distinction in approach to understanding and interpreting the Bible, and therefore to biblical authority. Walton quite thoroughly rejects the idea of concordism in his work on the Old Testament, and Ross similarly rejects Walton's approach to scripture. Here is Ross's explanation of the differences:

"Similar to all of us at RTB, Walton declares his belief in the inspiration and inerrancy of the Bible. However, the manner in which he sustains his belief is quite different from ours. Rather than seeing the Bible as full of content about the origin, history, and present state of the natural realm, Walton sees such content as being limited to what Old Testament authors knew from ancient Near Eastern literature and culture. This perspective is consistent with Walton's academic career at Wheaton, which was built upon numerous books and articles interpreting the Old Testament in light of ancient Near Eastern literature and culture.
In The Lost World Walton takes this limited scientific revelation interpretation of the Bible to an extreme and writes, 'Israelites received no revelation to update or modify their "scientific" understanding of the cosmos' (p. 16). Walton also asserts, "Through the entire Bible, there is not a single instance in which God revealed to Israel a science beyond their own culture. No passage offers a scientific perspective that was not common to the Old World science of antiquity" (p. 19)."

Let's agree for the moment that Moses is the author of Genesis. The difference in viewpoint is whether or not Moses, in the act of writing the words, was given access to knowledge about the nature of the universe that went beyond what he could possibly have known as a member of his time and culture. Most believe the Bible contains prophetic passages where humans were given access to future events and predicted accurately what would happen, including those passages that describe the coming of Jesus, his death and resurrection. But, does the Bible also contain "prophetic facts," or accurate descriptions (when properly interpreted) that are in concord with what science reveals to us? Walton says categorically "no." Ross offers a qualified "yes."

6. Head in the sand.

The final way of dealing with apparent factual contradictions from science is probably the most common, particularly among committed, thinking Christians. It's a hard question. As the effort at categorization here makes plain, there are no easy answers. Besides, there are kids to feed, a job to attend to, studies to complete and life goes on whether or not we figure out exactly what the meaning of inspiration is in relation to science. So, let's just put those questions aside and use the Bible for where we find its true value: in providing guidance for our daily lives and hope for an eternal future.

It's not an unreasonable approach. But, ultimately we have to accept that dealing with these difficult questions does matter. It matters particularly when we find ourselves praying and a small voice insists on interrupting our prayers saying things like, "you know perfectly well that no one is listening, so why go through this meaningless exercise?" And, "What God are you praying to today? The God of the vast universe and quantum mysteries, or the God of Moses who bent down in the mud and formed Adam? You know they are not the same." Leaving these questions untouched, for some at least, is distinctly unsatisfying because it leaves us torn, partial, incomplete, lacking integrity in the sense of not being whole. We long to be whole, to pray with confidence and integrity and our understanding of truth and meaning come from two contradictory sources we cannot be whole.

"Jesus loves me, this I know, for the Bible tells me so." Yes, but what if the Bible has it wrong? What if the Bible can't be trusted to tell the truth about the world, history, or life as it was and will be? The question is not academic. It is dreadfully real, personal and filled with consequence.

I mentioned earlier that at one time or another I can be found in almost all of those camps--except the strict inerrancy of Lindsell. My own way through this morass of authority is based on two simple ideas: all truth is God's truth, and continuing inspiration.

God is no post-modern in my understanding. There are absolutes of which is he is the first. It may be true that our experience of time and space may be very relative, as Einstein demonstrated, but that does not make all truth relative. Imagine you are standing outside a room with closed doors and windows. One person standing next to you says the light in that room is on. The other says, no it isn't. Let's leave Schrodinger's Cat and Everett's many world ideas out of it for the moment. I say, one of the fellows next to me is right and the other is wrong. There's really no middle ground. Either God is, or he isn't. I can't accept the nonsense of saying he's real for me but that doesn't mean he's real for you. Which also means there is such a thing as facts and truth. Either the world is approximately 13.7 billion years old, or it is not. Either life involved an act of will and intention, or it did not. It's hard for me to see how you can have some of these things both ways. And that means that there are those who are right about the nature of the world and the understanding of scripture and there are those who are wrong.

Continuing inspiration means to me that God continues to use the words contained in the Bible to communicate with those whose hearts and minds are open to such communication. The Lindsell approach to inerrancy is similar to the Islamic fundamentalist view of the Koran. The actual words are God's which means that the Koran can only be truly read in Arabic as that was the language Allah used to record the words. I don't buy this extreme literalist view of the Bible. But I do buy the idea that the Bible uniquely contains "the Word of God." That word is not about science and history, but about us, who we are, who he is, what kind of relationship he wants and expects from us. Continuing inspiration means that the mystery of God transmitting his thoughts and ideas to us is based not just on his role in the writing of the words, but in his role, his Spirit's role to be theologically precise, in you or me reading those words. That's why I think it is perfectly understandable that someone could read it and get no truth from it at all, no message from God, no deeper understanding of who they are and their relationship with the Author. But others read and it knocks them to their knees hearing, in some cases for the first time, the wonderful words of life. The Spirit, in this view, was alive at the writing, the translating, the editing, the redacting, and finally in the reading and comprehension.

Chapter 9
Legacy: On the Shoulder of Giants

It is part of human experience to think that we are alone in whatever we are experiencing. We tend to think we are the first and only to truly see a spectacular sunset, to feel a sudden terror that chills you to the bone, to wonder at the gnawing emptiness that sometimes grows inside us like we are made of mud. If you've ever watched first time new parents closely, it is quite clear that as far as they are concerned, the wonder they have given birth to is the first such creature in the whole world.

C. S. Lewis in *The Four Loves* defined friendship as what happens when we discover that others share something important to us. "What, you too?" one would exclaim in discovering that there was someone who shared something profound and meaningful.

As we consider the questions of science, faith, God and whether prayer has any meaning or not, it is normal to think our questions are new. We may have the sense that we are alone in contemplating the massive emptiness that confronts us as we stare past the clouds into the ever-deepening blue of space. Is anyone out there? Is anyone listening? Does anyone really care?

But, we are not alone in asking these questions. As we explore the questions raised and answers given by great minds who have gone before, we will find ourselves saying, "What? You too?" Consider how Epictetus, a Roman philosopher teaching Stoic philosophy in exile from Rome in Greece described the categories of belief in God:

"With respect to gods, there are some who say that a divine being does not exist; others that say that it exists, but is inactive and careless, and takes no forethought about anything; a third

class say that such a being exists and exercises forethought, but only about great things and heavenly things, and about nothing on earth; a fourth class say that a divine being exercises forethought both about things on the earth and heavenly things, but in a general way only, and not about things severally. There is a fifth class to whom Ulysses and Socrates belong, who say: 'I move not without thy knowledge.'"
—Iliad, x.,278

A contemporary translation of these five categories designed for easy consumption might look like this:

Five Classes of Belief in God as Understood by the Greeks

1. God does not exist
2. God exists but does not care
3. God cares only about great things and heaven
4. God cares about heavenly and earthly things, but not about us individually
5. God cares and is intimately involved in each of our lives

At one time or another my own beliefs have corresponded to each of these classes, although by upbringing, inclination and much consideration for the most of my life I fit into the class occupied by Ulysses and Socrates. That sounds ridiculously arrogant, until I think about the arrogance of so many outspoken atheists who continue to treat any form of belief as clear evidence of intellectual or emotional disability, or more likely, both. Their disdain for believers of all kinds in an age of science and secularism seems to ignore the fact that by far the majority of the greatest thinkers of all time shared a belief in God. In Socrates and Ulysses' case, a belief in a very personal and very involved God. I should note that Ulysses is the Roman name for Odysseus, a likely fictional Greek king featured in Homer's poem, "Odyssey." So, it may be more right to say Homer's belief, or Homer's depiction of the belief of his character.

Many orthodox believers might be surprised, shocked even, to discover how much of what we consider uniquely Christian teaching has come to us through other cultures and civilizations. This should not be as surprising as it is, but the fact that we are so ignorant of the sources of our cherished beliefs reflects poorly on the education of far too many Christian preaches and teachers. Teaching about the physical resurrection of the body is one example. There were very few references to any sort of meaningful life after death, either in spiritual or physical form, until late in the Old Testament. Even in Jesus' time, the wealthy leaders of Israel, the Sadducees, held to the idea that there is no form of life after death. Daniel, writing from exile in Babylon writes clearly about the resurrection of the body in Daniel 12. He may have been influenced in this by Persian culture and its primary religion at the time of the exile.

That may surprise many Christians. How many times has it been taught in a Christian education class that the ideas of heaven and hell didn't really develop in Jewish, and therefore pre-Christian thought, until during and after the exile? Daniel was the earliest biblical writer to have much to say about heaven, hell and bodily resurrection. He was a ruler in the Babylonian kingdom that held the Jewish people in exile. Many scholars believe that Daniel was influenced by the Persian culture and its religion called Zoroastrianism which had innovated the ideas of heaven and hell and personal judgment based on an individual's life of good or evil.

Paul, for his part, was an educated man. Educated in Jewish theology by the famed rabbi Gamaliel, but like all educated men of that time, he was deeply steeped in Hellenistic or ancient Greek culture and philosophy. That influence not only seeped into his creative constructs of early Christian theology, it flooded them. Many have noted how Paul's ideas about the church, the gifts of the spirit, righteousness as clothing, even love as the greatest virtue have Greek origins. Even Paul's famous and powerful exclamation of our difficulty in seeing the truth through the veil of our earthly limitations was something he learned in some Greek philosophy class. Because Plato, writing about 400 BC, quoting Socrates, said,

"For there is no light of justice or temperance or any of the higher ideas which are precious to souls in the earthly copies of them: they are seen through a glass dimly.."

A key element of Greek thought was the soul/body duality which is something clearly taught by Paul and something that is accepted by virtually all believers. Our commonly accepted ideas of spirit, body (flesh), heaven, hell, resurrection and judgment which we believe to be inspired by God most certainly reflect an amalgam of Jewish, Greek and Persian ideas and innovations.

The point of all this is not to undermine the idea of inspiration, or to suggest that Christianity is a fundamentally Greek or Persian faith, but rather to help us deal with the discomfort of confronting the apparent conflicts between what we have understood the bible to teach and what science now makes clear to us. We are not alone in this struggle. We may think that dealing with these apparent conflicts is unique to our time or to our own spiritual journey, but reading what some of the great minds of science have said on this topic will make it clear that there is nothing new here.

Galileo is a name that is quickly raised whenever the conflict between faith and science emerges. To the scientifically minded, he is the best symbol of the backwardness of those holding to religion in the face of newly revealed scientific truth. It's true: his forced denial of his teaching about the earth revolving around the sun and not the other way around is a black mark on Christian intellectual history. But, as usual, the story is more complex than commonly understood. First, those who hold up Galileo as a hero of science should recall that Galileo, like Isaac Newton later, was a thoroughgoing believer. Yes, certainly a product of his time and culture as we are, but his basic understanding of God as creator of the universe was never in question. Second, the famed confrontation between Galileo and the Pope resulting in his recanting his belief in the earth orbiting the sun, was caused as much by his personal relationships with the Pope and power players in the papal court, his own impolitic personality, and the papal politics of the time which influenced the Pope into a get-tough position to solidify his authority. Galileo's book in which the Pope is presented as the simpleton seems an almost intentional strategy to cause the confrontation. The real shame is how long it took the Catholic Church to make a formal admission of its error—such is the conservative nature of major institutions particularly when issues of infallibility are at stake.

Galileo knew his Bible. He knew the passages that talk about the sun revolving around the earth. He certainly was aware of the miracle of the sun standing still for Joshua so the commander could complete his victory and secure the promised land for God's chosen people. He believed, as most everyone did at that time, that the words were directly inspired by God. So the evidence of the earth's solar revolution so plainly clear to him through his calculations and telescope caused conflict. His resolution of that can be a powerful guide for all believers struggling with these questions today, even though our telescopes and calculations are many times more revealing of truth than Galileo's.

As quoted by Mark Noll, in *Jesus Christ and the Life of the Mind,* Galileo says,

"It is most pious to say and most prudent to take for granted that Holy Scriptures can never lie, as long as its true meaning has been grasped; but I do not think one can deny that this is frequently recondite and very different from what appears to be the literal meaning of the words...I think that in disputes about natural phenomena one must begin not with the authority of scriptural passage but with sensory experience and necessary demonstrations. For the Holy Scripture and nature derive equally from the godhead, the former as the dictation of the Holy Spirit and the latter as the most obedient executrix of God's orders;

more over, to accommodate the understanding of the common people it is appropriate for Scripture to say many things that are different (in appearance and in regard to the literal meaning of the words) from the absolute truth; on the other hand, nature is inexorable and immutable, never violates the terms of the laws imposed upon her, and does not care whether or not her recondite reasons and ways of operating are disclosed to human understanding; but not every scriptural assertion is bound to obligations as severe as every natural phenomenon; finally God reveals Himself to us no less excellently in the effects of nature than in the sacred words of Scripture…and so it seems that a natural phenomenon which is placed before our eyes by sensory experience should not be called into question, let alone condemned on account of scriptural passages whose words appear to have a different meaning."

It's worth underscoring some of Galileo's thoughts. He says in the disputes or conflicts of the kind we have been talking about, we should begin with "sensory experience and necessary demonstrations." Is this because nature is right and scripture wrong? No, it is because as he says the laws imposed on nature are fixed and dependable whether we understand them or not, but scripture is not bound to "obligations as severe as every natural phenomenon." That does not mean that scripture is less true than nature, but that the truth may be more obscure due to our own weakness in understanding and the fact that scripture was written in a time of limited scientific understanding. Because of this limitation, Galileo says that "it is appropriate for Scripture to say many things that are different (in appearance and in regard to the literal meaning of the words) from the absolute truth." So he concludes, if we are confronted with an apparent conflict between what nature is revealing as truth and we understand scripture to be saying, look first to our faulty understanding of scriptural truth. Do not let our faulty and weak understanding of scriptural truth discount the plain evidence of God's truth presented to us through our "sensory experience and necessary demonstrations."

Believers holding to a high view of scriptural literalism and direct inspiration will find such thinking excessively modern. Galileo, they may conclude, was too much of a liberal for them even though these thoughts are about 500 years old. But, another five hundred years or so before Galileo, another great teacher who believed in the scriptures, at least the Hebrew scriptures, said very much the same thing. Alister McGrath, writing in *Science and Religion: A New Introduction*, says that Maimonides, the great medieval Jewish philosopher, also taught that conflicts should be resolved by accepting the scientific truths and examining our scriptural interpretations in the light of those truths. McGrath says Maimonides, "who went so far as to suggest that if science and biblical interpretation were found to be in tension, this was because the science was not understood properly, or the biblical text was being misinterpreted. If science demanded certain beliefs that did not contradict any fundamentals of faith, then those beliefs should be accepted, and scripture interpreted in their light." Maimonides lived from 1153 to 1204.

Sir Isaac Newton arguably has contributed as much as any to our understanding of the workings of nature. As a non-orthodox Christian believer, he saw the profound discoveries he made in the laws of motion and calculus as clear evidence of a Designer. The laws he discovered did more to transform our ideas about the nature of creation than perhaps any other discovery. Newton saw in those laws the predictability and reliability necessary for the universe to work but also the nature of the Designer who would create such laws. He also understood that Moses, in writing Genesis and the account of creation, was writing to the "vulgar," his seventeenth century way of describing the people of Moses' time who did not have access to the same level of understanding of nature as Newton or those of his time did.

"As to Moses, I do not think his description of ye creation either philosophical or feigned, but that he described realities in a language artificially adapted to ye sense of ye vulgar. Thus when he speaks of two great lights, I suppose he means their apparent not real greatness. So when he tells us God placed these lights in ye firmament, he speaks I suppose of their apparent not real place, his business being not to correct the vulgar notions in matters philosophical, but to adapt a description of the creation as handsomely as he could to ye sense and capacity of ye vulgar. So when he tells us of two great lights, and ye stars made ye 4th day, I do not think their creation from beginning to end was done the 4th day, nor in any one day of ye creation, nor that Moses mentions their creation, as they were physicall bodies in themselves, some of them greater than the earth, and perhaps habitable worlds, but only as they were lights to this earth, so therefore though their creation could not physically [be] assigned to any one day, yet being a part of ye sensible creation which it was Moses's design to describe, and it being his design to describe things in order according to the succession of days, allotting no more than one day to one thing, they were to be referred to some day or other, and rather to the 4th day than any other, if they [the] air then first became clear enough for them to shine thro' it, and so put ye appearance of lights in ye firmament to enlighten the earth..."

Moses, Newton concludes, writing to the people of his time, described realities in a language adapted to the understanding of his audience. Consequently, as Newton describes in some detail about the creation of light, the actual words do not correspond perfectly to contemporary understandings of the world. Newton does not really comment on whether or not as part of God's inspiration that Moses had access to a higher level of knowledge that he was forced to contain for the sake of his audience. Or whether Moses' language was artificially constrained by his own limited knowledge. The suggestion is clear that the construct of seven days to describe creation is not intended by Moses to be literally understood, but that it was his "design to describe things in order according to the succession of days."

Augustine was one of the greatest thinkers the Christian community ever generated. Writing less than 400 years after the resurrection of Christ, already Augustine was dealing with the conflict between what educated and thinking non-believers knew about the nature of the world and what Christian believers understood the Bible to teach. It was clear he was concerned about this conflict, but for perhaps a surprising reason. His concern that faithful adherence to a false understanding of scripture could seriously undermine the credibility of those holding to those untenable positions, and therefore limit their effectiveness in communicating the far more important truths of Christian doctrine. In other words, if a non-believer knew perfectly well that the earth based on solid evidence was round, but confronted a believer who believed it was flat based on the words of scripture in contradiction to indisputable evidence, what would that non-believer think about scripture? Here is the concern as expressed by Augustine:

"If they [the educated non-believer] find a Christian mistaken in a field which they themselves know well and hear him maintaining his foolish opinions about our books, how are they going to believe those books in matters concerning the resurrection of the dead, the hope of eternal life, and the kingdom of heaven, when they think their pages are full of falsehoods on facts which they themselves have learnt from experience and the light of reason?"

This is a very clear and present danger for the Christian faith in our time. There can be little doubt that the Christian message has lost much of its power and credibility within the greater world because of the denial of clearly established facts. We don't live on a flat earth; we don't live in a universe where the earth is at the very center. We do live in a world of a Big Bang, of quantum theory, of evolutionary processes. To hold firmly to outdated understandings of a world based on faulty interpretations of scripture has the inevitable impact of making scripture look foolish and outdated when it is the interpreters who are. Mark Noll in *Jesus Christ and the Life of the Mind*, makes clear how strongly Augustine felt about this potentially tragic mistake:

"His closing injunction was to chastise 'reckless and incompetent expounders of Holy Scripture' who 'defend their utterly foolish and obviously untrue statements' by calling on 'Holy Scripture for proof and even recit[ing] from memory many passages which they think support their position."

Those who struggle with this issue of authority -- biblical authority versus scientific authority -- should take comfort that this struggle is not new. Great minds have confronted these critical issues beginning, no doubt, with the very idea of inspired scripture. Warnings without end have been issued by the faithful of the dangers of straying too far from the tried and previously true interpretations. It is time, perhaps, to take some warning from those who make clear the danger of not taking established scientific truth seriously.

Chapter 10
Metaphysic: Spiritual and Material Realities

What is natural, and what is supernatural? Everyone seems to know the answer to that. Natural things are subject to the known laws of nature and don't vary from them. Supernatural things are those outside of scientific evidence. They are undetectable and most certainly supernatural if they violate the laws of nature. The fact that this understanding is one of the most common among most in our world is a stunning victory for Enlightenment ideas. This fundamental remaking of our understanding of the world coincided with and was created in part by the emergence of science as the most reliable determiner of truth and testable facts in and of our world. The very clear distinction between what is natural and supernatural, physical and metaphysical, real and imagined, is part of our cultural soup -- our shared mental framework of the world. A fish giving thought to the fact that it exists in water is not too dissimilar from us giving thought to the idea that maybe the distinction between nature and supernature is not correct.

But I am going to ask you to be the fish thinking about the water it is in for a bit.

It does not take much study of the intellectual history of human beings to see that this idea of the clear separation of nature and super-nature is both new and unique. Throughout human history neither the common ordinary peasant nor the most profound philosophers considered this distinction. We, in our "enlightened" state have long considered this to clearly demonstrate our superiority in knowledge of the world. We reduced anything outside of what is proven science to the categories of the occult, the weak-minded, the weird, the untrustworthy, the unthinking religious.

While this is still very much a dominant element of our cultural soup or the water we swim in, it does seem this distinction is breaking down. While I believe most in the sciences, and particularly the fundamentalist atheists intent on evangelizing their beliefs, will vehemently disagree, a review of the many varied wild, crazy, fantastic, speculative and totally unproven beliefs of today's physicists and scientists may well prove my point. What is now being seriously studied as legitimate scientific investigation further proves my point. The implications for how we think about the world, God, our place in it and yes, prayer and its effectiveness are very significant.

But before looking at what science teaches us today let's look at how what is considered natural keeps changing.

The sun brilliantly filled my east facing windows this morning, and last night we once again enjoyed a brilliant red sunset as the sun settled down against the San Juan Islands in northwest Washington state. Sometimes I try to imagine the natural reality of the earth spinning at this latitude at about 750 miles per hour and the sun stationary (not really as it speeds around the Milky Way, but stationary from earth's perspective) rather than rising and falling as it certainly appears. That rising and falling is perfectly natural, not supernatural. But it was not always seen that way. The Greeks saw it as Apollo riding his flaming chariot across the sky. How could anyone doubt or question when the god made his regular, daily appearance with such magnificent evidence?

The sun rising and falling are no longer supernatural, neither is the rainbow, or thunder and lightning for that matter. A month after I graduated from high school there were men walking on the moon. If I had had the chance to talk to my great-grandfather and told him there were men walking on the moon, do you think, assuming he believed me, that it was natural? If I told my grandmother, born near the turn of the twentieth century, when she was still a child that by the time she died there would be more than half a million souls whizzing around the sky at over 30,000 feet at any moment of the day, would she think I was talking crazy or supernatural? Speaking of supernatural, did you ever watch a 747 takeoff?

I chopped down a giant sunflower yesterday, and thought about the growth of that monstrous plant from one small seed. Then I thought about a baby being born from the union of a barely visible egg with an invisible sperm. That is natural, but can you blame most of humankind for tens or hundreds of thousands of years for thinking that there was something supernatural about it? We dismiss these things as if with a wave of the hand. Oh, that's natural. It's just part of the order of things. It's just a process following completely predictable, reliable laws. There is something lost in this process of going from supernatural to natural, something magical, fantastical, mysterious and romantic. But, it must happen because now we know better. These are merely natural events and processes, nothing special about them.

If we look to the past as our guide it is not remarkable to think that what we now consider supernatural will quite possibly be considered natural in the future. Michio Kaku, well-known physicist and educator, has written a book called *Physics of the Impossible: A Scientific Exploration into the World of Phasers, Force Fields, Teleportation, and Time Travel.* He very rationally explores how most of these and related topics which we consider to be physically impossible are really not. Contemporary physics is blurring the lines of the natural and supernatural by claiming the supernatural ground as natural.

The field of the supernatural, including the field of God's activity, has narrowed considerably in the past two hundred years. Newton showed that the planets stay in their orbits not by the direct hand of God but by gravity and inertia. The inexorable advance of science has continually intruded into the realm that once was attributed to God. Believers have often resisted this advance because there is a natural inclination to rely on the evidence of God's activity in the world as solid proof of his existence. But, the fundamentalist atheists who use science to promote their anti-theistic beliefs love to trumpet the victory of science over the action of God claiming that ultimately there will be no more gaps for God to fill. They may be right. But they may find when all the gaps are gone that they have done nothing more than uncovered the deeper mysteries of God and his actions.

Think for a moment of what you consider supernatural. The spirit world? Heaven? Hell? Purgatory? How about miracles? How about answers to prayer? Ghosts? Communicating with the dead? Devils and demons? Time travel? Warp speed? Levitation? Immortality? God him/herself?

My suggestion is clear, if startling: things we now consider supernatural will sometime, perhaps in the not too distant future, be considered natural. More than that, I am suggesting that the very recent artificial distinction between natural and supernatural is disappearing right before our eyes.

In early 2013 *Wired* magazine published an article about Dr. Sam Parnia who heads the resuscitation research program at Stony Brook University Hospital. In this capacity he has studied hundreds of cases of what is commonly-called "Near Death Experiences" but what he calls "After Death Experience." Consciousness, he has demonstrated, lasts beyond death. He says, "The evidence we have so far is that human consciousness does not become annihilated." The reason is that with advanced resuscitation, it is now possible to restore life to those who have died by every common definition, including the loss of all brain electrical activity. This is possible because doctors have discovered that cells, even brain cells, can remain viable for many hours after all blood flow has stopped. But, take note: though the brain cells may remain viable, in these cases brain activity has stopped. No more electrochemical activity, no more synapses, no thoughts, no memory recall, nothing. However, when such people are resuscitated, they report vivid experiences.

Parnia comments: "These observations raise a question about our current concept of how brain and mind interact. The historical idea is that electrochemical processes in the brain lead to consciousness. That may no longer be correct, because we can demonstrate that those processes don't go on after death. There may be something in the brain we haven't discovered that accounts for consciousness, or it may be that consciousness is a separate entity from the brain."

The reporter for the magazine, reflecting the naturalist bent of today's media, asks the pressing question: "This seems to verge on supernatural explanations of consciousness." To which Parnia gives a thoroughly scientific answer that also shows the bridging between natural and supernatural:

"Throughout history, we try to explain things the best we can with the tools of science. But most open-minded and objective scientists recognize that we have limitations. Just because something is inexplicable with our current science doesn't make it superstitious or wrong. When people discovered electromagnetism, forces that couldn't then be seen or measured, a lot of scientists made fun of it. Scientists have come to believe that the self is brain cell processes, but there's never been an experiment to show how cells in the brain could possibly lead to human thought. If you look at a brain cell under a microscope, and I tell you, "this brain cell thinks I'm hungry," that's impossible. It could be that, like electromagnetism, the human psyche and consciousness are a very subtle type of force that interacts with the brain, but are not necessarily produced by the brain. The jury is still out."

The study of consciousness and of near death or after death experiences is just one of many areas where scientific study is impinging on the formerly forbidden borders of metaphysics and the supernatural. Here are a few other examples:

The many dimensions of reality

We believe mostly in three dimensions of space, which we can express as height, depth and width. Most now add a fourth dimension: time. It is only barely possible to imagine life in two dimensions. All of life would exist as on a flat panel TV screen or a flat plane. You could move forward, backward, across but not up or down. There would be no depth. Now imagine living in a reality with ten dimensions, or eleven. Where would they be? Where would you go? How would the objects that we encounter in everyday life be different? Yet, the predominant theory of how to tie gravity and classical physics with the Standard Model (the other three forces of nature) and quantum mechanics together is string theory, which today requires ten or eleven dimensions. Sure, they say that most of them are rolled up tight like a straw, but if you unrolled them like a straw they would be a plane—a flat, two dimensional spacetime element. Did I lose you? I'm lost too. The point is, this is what many if not most physicists and cosmologists believe about our world. Have they seen one of these rolled up dimensions? No, but their mathematics says they are there. Is there physical evidence? No, not as far as I can tell. You can't touch it, taste it, experience it, or measure it. But you can prove it to be there by the pure thought process known as mathematics. I want to ask, does merely thinking about something make it real, even if it can't be submitted to the Testability Principle?

Physical singularities

Singularities are now commonly accepted in physics. A singularity is the answer to the question of where all the matter in the universe came from before the Big Bang. Before the massive explosion that was the moment of Creation, matter was contained in a single, infinitely small point. Smaller than a grain of sand--trillions of times smaller-- yet it contained within it the makings of everything there is. Singularities are also those things at the center of black holes. A black hole is created when a star dies and collapses on itself under the sheer force of gravity. Black holes have so much mass and therefore exert so much gravitational force that nothing, not even massless light, can escape their pull. Hence, black hole. That has to be a lot of mass, but again it is condensed into a single, incredibly small point, or line if the black hole is rotating. How much mass? As much as fifty billion suns. That's what some are calculating as the biggest possible black hole. One has been found that contains 18 billion suns. The sun is pretty massive. Imagine putting the earth on a bathroom scale and weighing it. How much more would the sun weigh? 332,000 times. You'd have to pile 332,000 earths on top of that scale to get to the mass of the sun. Now, try to think for a moment about 18, or even 50, billion suns. Let's start with a hundred. That's a lot. Now try one thousand suns. OK, try a million. A million suns would be really, really warm, and big. Now multiply that million by a thousand, one thousand million. That's one billion. Now, multiply that times eighteen. Now put those 18 billions suns, or their equivalent mass, into your pocket, or a speck of dust, or a speck on a speck. Our minds can't really go there. But today's physics can. This is not speculation, this is real. It's not supernatural, its nature according to contemporary physics.

Fine-tuning coincidence

"Thank our lucky stars" is a common phrase with extra meaning today. Fate and good luck would generally fall into the supernatural category, similar to providence. The difference is whether you attribute the good or bad fortune received as a result of blind forces beyond us or some Intelligence that plans it. Coincidence is the name given for happenings that are so unusual that they appear to be intended or planned, but by attributing them to coincidence they move into the realm of the natural world vs. supernatural. These things just happen without needing explanation. It's a matter of probability and probability is determined by how many options there are. However, most scientists believe in a coincidence that they would rationally say is impossible. It's the coincidence, or rather the remarkable series of tightly interconnected coincidences, that constitute fine-tuning. As some would say, it seems clear the universe intended for us to be here. It "knew" we were coming. But for the universe to have a will, intention, or knowledge is no longer natural, it is supernatural. Certainly for the universe to be caused by intention or design is supernatural. The only way strident non-theists have of dealing with the untenable coincidence of fine-tuning is the multiverse option. There had to have been enough universes to come into existence all on their own for one of them to have the conditions so spectacularly just right for life, let alone human life. That constitutes belief in something that is unproven, untested and potentially beyond testing. Most of the people who believe in the multiverse as a strategy for avoiding God would say anyone who believes in ideas beyond measurement and testing accepts the supernatural. And that of course means that they do.

Quantum observation

We've talked about quantum observation and the strange conclusion suggested by this reality. The idea that God spoke and the chaos of the world was brought into order is considered supernatural activity at its highest. But how different is this from the idea that merely by observing the location of a particle, a conscious mind changes it, reducing all its unlimited potential locations, momentum and histories into one, single reality? And that without that conscious mind that particle stays forever in a "superposition" state, existing anywhere and everywhere at all times. But that is what some believe contemporary physics teaches. Others, who don't believe that explanation, have few other rational explanations as alternatives. How can a conscious mind have such an impact on the position and history of one particle, and from that, all interconnected particles? To try and describe this pushes the boundaries of the supernatural, but the effect is exceptionally well established, even if the mechanism causing it remains mysterious and controversial.

Dark energy and matter

Traditional believers believe in supernatural realities such as the Holy Spirit. It's an invisible force with, to believers, demonstrable results. But it resists laboratory tests and is not directly observable. Sort of sounds like how scientists believe in dark matter and dark energy. No one has "found" dark matter or energy, subjected it to close inspection in the lab, or even proven definitively that it exists. Yet, few scientists doubt its existence. It seems our world could not exist without these dark and mysterious entities.

Gravity is a certain and inexorable force. In other words, we can count on it to always do what it does which is to pull items that have mass toward each other. That includes things like gigantic galaxies and stars to the smallest particles. So, if the universe began with a huge explosion called the "Big Bang, and the universe from its earliest moments included gravity, it would be logical to assume that the expansion of the universe from the force of the Big Bang would eventually run out of steam. That's what the assumption was until the Hubble space telescope made it clear that our universe's expansion was accelerating rather than slowing. Further, this expansion started to accelerate inexplicably well into the history of the universe. There is no known cause for this expansion. NASA's website explains that there are now three possible explanations for this accelerating expansion: One, Maybe Einstein was right when he originally proposed the idea of a "cosmological constant," a number he threw out to make the math of gravity work out properly; two, maybe there is "some kind of strange energy-fluid that filled space; and three, maybe Einstein was wrong about gravity and a whole new theory is needed. Scientists don't know, but they are calling this mystery "dark energy."

Dark matter is pretty strange, too. Scientists really have very little idea of what it is, except they are quite certain that it exists. Again, explanations for our universe as it is observed don't work without this dark stuff. It's not made of the kind of particles that we include as our reality—not the stuff of us, our planet, our stars—anything recognizable. It is "dark" because we can't see it, that is, it resists all our current methods of observation. According to Wikipedia, most scientists believe that dark matter is made up of WIMPS—that is weakly interacting massive particles. These are just hypothetical things—nothing proven, yet. But if they are real, they can't be seen because they don't emit or absorb light or electromagnetic energy, but they interact through the weak force and gravity. They'd have to if they had mass. So, let's see. There are these things out there that have mass, lots and lots of mass, but you can't touch them, see them, measure them (other than weighing), and certainly can't figure out what they are or what they are made of.

This might not be so strange if these were just sort of sideshows to the universe, but it appears they are the main act. Dark matter and dark energy account for 85% of the total "stuff" of the universe. The normal matter that makes up our lives, our planet, and the incredibly huge, massive universe that causes us to marvel is just five per cent of the total!

The empty space of solids

What are you made of? Tissue, blood, bones. Solid things, right? What are they made of? Cells. Made up of chemical elements which are atoms arranged in specific ways called molecules. So what are atoms made of? The Greeks came up with the idea and name of atom, which means indivisible or un-cuttable, because they surmised that there must be some building block of all this stuff that was at the very bottom. Now we know that atoms are made up of many particles which we call elementary particles because they are supposedly the most basic. These include things like leptons and gluons and quarks with charm and up and down and all that. The search goes on and with the new Large Hadron Collider near Geneva. Switzerland, the expectation is that even more elementary particles might be found. Indeed, the Higgs Boson, the so-called "God Particle," is believed to have been identified by the massive collider in 2012.

While we see and experience most matter as solid, in reality it is anything but solid. First, there are the vast spaces in the world of atoms and sub-atomic particles. An atom is made up of a nucleus and electron whirling away around the nucleus. But if the nucleus were the size of a marble, the electron would be somewhere out there a few miles away. A few miles? That's a lot of empty space! What's in there? Empty space is what scientists tend to call anything they know exists, but don't know what it is or how to find it. As we know, a vacuum isn't just nothing. So that "empty space" that must make up 99.9% or more of everything we are, see and know, must be something.

But, then there is the strange fact that electrons like all particles have both particle and wave properties. A wave is not a particle—it's just a thing that influences other things over time and space. So, an electron as a wave is just kind of a fuzzy thing spinning around the nucleus, spewing out photons once in a while and in the process jumping from one orbit to another. To make it worse, we can't really locate it, or say how fast it is going, or say specifically where it is, unless we measure it -- like with some sort of conscious mind -- and then we can only know a certain amount about it.

So, that all sounds very insubstantial. But I know the computer I am writing on has keys that go down when the electrons that make up the flesh of my fingers come in contact with the electrons in the plastic of these keys. Why? And why is this cheap plastic table holding up this computer quite reliably, like these cheap plastic chairs I'm sitting on? If everything is clouds, fuzzy, indeterminate, all over the place at once, why do we experience reality as something solid and reliable?

One key is the Pauli Exclusion principle that says basically there is a law of the universe that two electrons cannot be found in the same time and place in the universe at the same time. That means that despite the fact that electrons are vanishingly small (or just waves) and nuclei are also pretty tiny overall and you have all that space between them, this exclusionary principle says they can't share that empty space. It's sacred. No touch.

As I look at this screen, or my lovely wife or the mountains near our home I see them as solid. And solid means real. But in reality, I know that nothing is solid in that sense, it is all tiny bits of matter that are separated by vast distances of emptiness and that the matter itself is nothing more than insubstantial clouds of energy. We have eyes tuned to see it as we think it is. We don't see clouds of space and tiny particles that make up what we now know to be real. What if we had eyes tuned to see as it really was? What if our eyes could see all that empty space, those tiny bits matter floating around at vast distances from each other? What if our eyes could see whatever it is that is constituting dark matter -- the stuff that now evades all our ability to measure and observe? More, what if we had eyes tuned to see the reality of God?

Quantum fluctuations and virtual particles

We think of empty space as a vacuum where nothing exists and nothing happens. Not so. At any point in such a place energy levels may change quite on their own. It's called quantum fluctuations. It also means that particles (matter and energy are interchangeable remember) can pop into and out of existence in this "empty space." Presumably, this means the empty space in those "miles" between the neutrons and electrons that make up the atoms that make up my body. These "particles" pop into existence and out of existence with great speed. The longer they hang around, the more like a real or non-virtual particle they become. The force of these particles and quantum fluctuation has been measured, and indeed, this fact of nature plays a role in designing today's computer chips and nanotechnology. Some even think that the creation of the universe was a matter of a quantum fluctuation or virtual particle popping into existence and starting the whole ball rolling.

No doubt any theological speculation on the impact of these fluctuations or virtual particles would be dismissed with a guffaw by the naturalist types. However, if they are measurable and have force, it seems quite expected that they could even in small ways change the reality that we experience. Might it not be possible to find someday that through the agency of virtual particles we find that some force, some intentional consciousness, affected our thoughts, our actions, our futures? Sure, that's metaphysical speculation but the very idea of little bits of matter appearing out of nowhere and near nothingness, then disappearing into nowhere and nothingness doesn't sound very much like hard-headed science.

Inflation theory or how our universe came to be the way it is

Nothing goes faster than the speed of light. It's the cosmic speed limit. As we saw earlier, the only exception is this strange phenomenon of quantum entanglement in which particles once connected stay connected instantaneously no matter how far distant they are. But, there is the other exception and without it, we couldn't exist. It's called "inflation theory."

We can sort of understand the idea of the Big Bang. In the beginning, there was nothing. Then there was this tiny tiny thing called the singularity and it exploded. And all the stuff in the singularity got flung out from the huge explosion and from that our stars, galaxies, planets and eventually us, evolved. But, there was a problem with that. The universe as observed didn't fit the model. The universe has structure and a shape that couldn't exist based simply on the physics of the Big Bang. So in 1980 American physicist Alan Guth proposed "inflation" as the answer. (Might it have been called that because economic inflation was big at the time?) In the very first moments of the Big Bang, this idea says that forces beyond our understanding flung out the universe at a rate far faster than anything we can imagine. Inflation occurred between 10^{-36} and 10^{-33} or 10^{-32} seconds after the Big Bang. That's not much time. That's a ten with 36 zeroes behind it. But in that blinding flash of time, the universe expanded by 10^{78} in volume—that's ten with 78 zeroes behind it. That's big.

It seems it takes huge leaps of imagination, far beyond anything contemporary science can prove, to come up with such ideas. Yet this idea is widely accepted as the most reasonable explanation for the mysteries of the uniformity and structure of our universe. The search of scientists, as always, is to come up explanations as to how things can be as they are without some sort of guiding hand doing it. Inflation theory is one possible answer to the extremely difficult question of how natural processes could account for the universe as it is. There is a problem, however. For inflation to occur, as Roger Penrose points out, the initial conditions had to be even more specific. In other words, the fine-tuning problem becomes even more intense with inflation—how could such a wonderful coincidence just happen? And there is the other problem: if inflation is simply following the laws of physics, where did they come from? As quoted by Nichols in *The Sacred Cosmos*, Guth said: "Even in this state the laws of physics would have to exist, and their origin is a mystery."

Multiverse and Every Eventuality as Reality

I have saved the best for last. We have made reference many times to the multiverse. This is the idea that our universe is not alone, as vast as it is. It is one of many, many universes, perhaps all connected so that our universe is like a bubble or a tumor on a much vaster balloon. There are a few reasons why this idea has gained so much popularity. One, it is the only possible explanation for fine-tuning other than theism. Since a theistic answer to the question of the origin of the universe and the laws of physics that guide it would be throwing in the scientific towel to many scientists, another explanation has to be found. No God of the gaps allowed—even this, the biggest of all gaps. Alan Lightman in *The Accidental Universe* explains: "Intelligent Design is an answer to fine-tuning that does not appeal to most scientists. The multiverse offers another explanation." Seemingly, the only other possible explanation.

Another and somewhat related reason is String Theory. This is a very popular explanation for the way things are and is one of the most promising possibilities for providing the elusive "theory of everything" that links quantum mechanics to classical physics.

One development of string theory, the multiple-dimension M-theory mathematically calls for, or at least allows for, multiple universes.

The multiverse idea has also gained favor as it relates to quantum theory. Developed initially by Hugh Everett III in 1957, it provides an answer to the intriguing question of quantum mechanics and the superposition or eigenstate of particles. You may recall that it looks very much like that until observed by a conscious mind, particles exhibit both their wave and particle natures and exist in an undetermined state. We don't know if they are here or there and we don't know how fast they are going. The observation "collapses" this state into something measurable. Because of this, as Richard Feynman showed, each particle has an infinite number of histories. A particle's collapse could impact the tornado hitting the midwest (recall the butterfly effect), it could alter the DNA of an unborn child, it could change how the president of the United States thought about how to respond to an international crisis. All these histories are possible. But in the Many Worlds interpretation of Everett, these are not just possible, they are real. Every possible thing that can happen because of the collapse of a particle does happen, is happening, will happen. It just depends on the particular universe you are inhabiting. Remember Schrodinger's cat which he demonstrated had to be both alive and dead using quantum theory? Well, the Many Worlds interpretation says, of course, in one universe the cat is alive and in the other one it is dead. Whether you see it as alive or dead depends on the universe you are in.

You may think at this point that I am joking. I'm not. Brian Cox is one of the most popular popularizers of contemporary science. He and Jeff Forshaw published a book in 2011 which we referenced earlier called *Quantum Universe: Everything That Can Happen Does Happen*.

These respected scientists, writers and broadcasters, are promoting this idea not as a far-fetched wild-eyed theory, but as the accepted science of the day. And so it is.

Lightman in *The Accidental Universe* is honest in admitting that this idea of the multiverse disturbs many scientists. Regarding the multiverse:

"There is no way they can prove this conjecture. That uncertainty also disturbs many physicists who are adjusting to the idea of the multiverse. Not only must we accept that basic properties of our universe are accidental and uncalculable. In addition, we must believe in the existence of many other universes. But we have no conceivable way of observing these other universes and cannot prove their existence. Thus, to explain what we see in the world and in our mental deductions, we must believe in what we cannot prove. Sound familiar? Theologians are accustomed to taking some beliefs on faith. Scientists are not. Such arguments, in fact, run hard against the long grain of science."

There is irony in many scientists taking the extreme measure of proposing a fantastic idea for which there can be conceivable proof, then taking it on faith -- all to avoid the "foolishness" of those who take the idea of God on faith.

Jim Baggott, one contemporary science writer who has the nerve to call a spade and spade and suggest that scientists, in their effort to avoid non-scientific explanations, have resorted to non-scientific explanations. In *Farewell to Reality*, he says:

"Finally, and most importantly, we must be concerned about the implications of multiverse theories for the future development of science itself. The multiverse theorists know they are on weak ground regarding the Testability Principle, and rather than admit that their theories are not science, they argue instead that the rules of science must be adapted to accommodate this kind of metaphysical speculation."

Another irony of this extreme approach to explain fine-tuning and the measurement problem is that ultimately, the multiverse is no sure way to get rid of God. What if it is real? Despite the hopes of the fundamentalist naturalists, it does not do away with the need for a Creator because where did the multiverse come from? The quantum vacuum? More nonsensical non-science says Baggott. More than that, as my son Geoff has pointed out repeatedly, the multiverse would prove the existence of God. If all possible realities are indeed realities then since God is a possible reality he is indeed a reality. In some universe. Perhaps its the ultimate irony that the scientists taking these desperate measures to avoid God are in the very universe he inhabits.

I will leave it to a physicist and science writer, Marcelo Gleiser, who in a blog post on NPR in late 2012 summed up the primary argument here of the blending of the natural and supernatural:

"Our philosophies, our sciences and religions are attempts to comprehend who we are in spite of our shortsightedness, of the limited ways that we see and understand what's going on. In this search, it's no surprise that religious belief works as a compass to so many people. How to explain the origin of the universe? Or of life? Or why life ends? How to explain why we have minds capable of reflecting about these kinds of complex questions? Or how the brain, taken as a bunch of neurons and synapses, manages to engender us with a sense of self? Of course, these questions are now part of cutting-edge scientific research. We live in a peculiar time, when what once was the province of religion is now part of science's daily goings-on."

He might add, and where the province of science has become strangely religious.

Chapter 11
Theology: What Difference Does It Make?

What does it matter? What does all this information, thinking, chit chat and argument about what science teaches or doesn't teach about God really matter? I bump into that question time and again and each time it frustrates me and nearly causes speechlessness -- a rare condition for me. The implication of the person asking that question is that all this is angel's dancing on the head of the pin stuff. Maybe fun for a few egghead types, but for the rest of us life will go on pretty much as normal and the fact that a few are discussing quantum fluctuations and the many worlds view of reality won't change a thing.

But, it matters because worldview matters. David Foster Wallace was called the most brilliant American writer of his generation. In 2005 he gave the graduation address at Kenyon College in Ohio. The speech has become one of the most famous of all graduation speeches and was published as a small book. It's called *This is Water: Some Thoughts, Delivered On a Significant Occasion, About Living a Compassionate Life.* Living a compassionate life, Wallace taught, was about understanding the "water" we swim in. The story he told about a conversation among fish suggests how difficult it is to understand the cultural environment that is our water. Fish cannot conceive of water. We find it almost as difficult to understand that our worldview, social structures and cultural norms largely drive who we are, how we think, what decisions we make and how we live our lives.

Take naturalism versus theism. If you take the idea of God seriously, particularly in the traditional Jewish, Christian and Muslim teaching that he is relational, involved and that he judges, then how you live your life will reflect that belief or worldview. If you have a strong sense that at the end you will stand before a holy and non-appealable magistrate who holds your immortal future in his hands, you will give a thought to that at least occasionally when you make decisions about how you live your life. On the other hand, if you subscribe to a thoroughly naturalist view then life ends when the brain cells die, you rot in the grave like the rest of carbon-based life and the only basis for making any decisions about right or wrong is the selfish gene. To make any decisions based on some intuitive sense of right and wrong is simply not coherent. You would live life with a clear understanding that your inner sense of purpose and meaning was some sort of evolutionary trick, is pure deception and is wisely ignored.

The plain fact is that most who subscribe to a more or less pure naturalist worldview still operate as if right and wrong matter, as if there is something purposeful and meaningful about life. This suggests that the dissonance I referred to in the first chapter is widespread among atheists and theists alike.

You've joined me in my meandering journey through contemporary science and what it has to say about God, reality and truth. This meandering journey has been profound for me in how it has challenged some dearly held ideas, deepened some convictions while weakening others. Most of all it has given me confidence for our future and enlivened my prayer life. Your journey may result in very different outcomes but I encourage you to try to articulate what your understanding of truth is and how that understanding affects how you think, behave and experience life. Writing is thinking for me. I don't really know what I think until I talk it through with someone or attempt, as I have done here, to capture what I think in words. If reading this book has done anything for you, I hope it has encouraged you to think through, preferably in words, what you really believe about these issues of God, life, who you are and what is really important.

Here is my attempt at such an explanation.

A God who is there

Does God really exist? I come firmly down on the side of belief, a confidence that has been strengthened greatly by reviewing contemporary science. As stated earlier, science will give both atheists and theists plenty of support for their chosen positions. Our predispositions greatly affect the way evidence is used by our minds. But those who reject God on the basis of contemporary science have a pretty steep hill to climb. You can decide the world is the result of design and hence a Designer given the reality of fine-tuning. But if you choose chance as the explanation rather than design you are forced into an equally unbelievable and un-provable infinity of universes. Chance requires it. The measurement problem of quantum particles provides an additional challenge. The only apparent alternative today to the possibility of the interaction of mind and matter at the quantum level is the many worlds theory in which all things that are possible are actual. But, as our son Geoff eagerly points out, if the many worlds theory is correct and all things that are possible are actual, then God is possible and that makes God real. Necessarily so. Unless God is not possible, of course. But then all things are possible except what you decide is impossible. Not coherent.

The universe is fine-tuned to a remarkable degree. Life evolved in ways that science so far has not shown any ability to explain. Humans with consciousness emerged and science is increasingly suggesting that consciousness is something beyond the computers made of meat we carry on our necks -- despite the heroic efforts of folks like Dennett and Kurzweil. The evidence toward theism was enough for a lifelong atheist such as Anthony Flew to change his mind, following the evidence where it led as he said he always did. The evidence led him to theism. The evidence is there for those who choose to see it. The burden of proof is clearly shifting and with it a cultural ferment equal to if not greater than the Enlightenment. The rantings of the new apostles of atheism only buttress the suggestion that the ground of this discussion is shifting. But that is my predisposition. What is yours?

A God who acts

Before starting this journey it seemed there were two options regarding God acting in this world: miracles or nothing. Our worldview accepted the idea of mechanism. The universe is a machine operating according to strict, immutable laws. The sun rises because the earth rotates, not because God says, Get up sun! God's action was left to miracles which were defined as breaking those immutable laws. Since there was little, if any, evidence that those laws were ever broken, only the credulous and extreme faithful could hold to miracles. This was and still is for many, the crucial dividing line in worldviews. Either you say laws of nature are violated at God's whim, science be damned, or you say miracles don't happen, period. And if miracles don't happen then the Bible isn't true and if there is a God, he's not the God of the Bible and surely doesn't mess with this world or us. God may create, in this view, but he does not answer personal prayer.

But now there is a coherent third way. I can, based on my understanding of contemporary science, see that God has great freedom to act in this universe without even coming close to violating any of these sacred laws of nature. Quantum uncertainty, the inability to distinguish between random action and intention, and the nature of complexity and chaos combine to make it entirely coherent to see how God can act without violation of the laws he himself put in place. Each of these by themselves could allow God to operate with freedom. Together they make it seem to me all but a certainty that he can and does.

Chaos, as we saw, says that in any complex system, the sheer number of things affecting the outcome makes the outcome unpredictable. Billiard balls on a table are the common example. Hit them with the cue ball, and after a certain number of bounces, what happens cannot be accurately predicted. Even a supercomputer of unimaginable computing power cannot determine it because the slightest change in conditions, a solar flare perhaps, or that mythical butterfly in Patagonia disturbing air molecules, can effect change even if it is miniscule. God can hide in those uncertainties. His action, so delicately applied, can have great impact in this kind of complex system.

Now add uncertainty to this chaos. Werner Heisenberg named the Uncertainty Principle when he found an unchangeable aspect of quantum particle behavior was that a particle's position and momentum cannot be observed at the same time. We can know where it is but not know its momentum or speed. We can know its speed but we can't know its position. This is due to the very fuzzy wave nature of quantum particles (which I remind you, constitute everything). The dual slit experiment demonstrates this. A particle operates like a wave or field spreading over vast distances with the properties of a wave such as frequency. But it also operates as a particle locatable at a certain point. Superposition means it's here, there and everywhere. Position means it's here and not there and everywhere. Some kind of measurement requiring, it appears to some at least, observation by a conscious mind, is what may be the only means of transition from position to superposition. Consciousness appears to be constructed so deeply into our world that everything in it cannot operate in the way we experience them as reality unless consciousness is there.

I may not have the science here perfectly correct and I'm certain that those who know far more about this than I do are cringing at my unschooled description. But the point is unmistakable: there is freedom to operate. Location, position, momentum, energy, spin are all aspects of quantum particles and they matter. Scientists believe in randomness, that is, much of what happens happens as a result of random actions of these particles. Random to a scientist means an absence of pattern. But such absence suggests that it is also without purpose, direction or intention. My question is this: how could a scientist tell whether an action was random or intended if it remains within the limits of how particles behave? Certainly, if enough "random" actions occur in a sequence and that pattern appears more than mere coincidence then wise minds will question whether it is truly random. Those who would hold firmly to randomness without any chance of undetectable intention may find it difficult to turn it around and defend "fine-tuning" as random. Is there any better example of pattern and non-randomness in the known laws of science? It seems to me that even the best scientist with the most advanced gear could not say definitively that the action of a particular particle or sequence of actions was 100% random rather than directed by an unseen Mind.

I'm not saying that God operates in the freedom of uncertainty and the complexity of chaos. I don't know. But it strikes me that it is very possible. And that means I can believe that God CAN act in our time and space without the slightest violation of the laws of nature. Can God affect weather? If the butterfly in South America beats his wings this second instead of two minutes from now, and that time gap affects the sun or rain, I suspect God can have something to say to that butterfly. Can God heal a deathly disease short of a miracle? With the complexity and uncertainty of our immune systems, with the difference of action in particles at the most elementary level, it certainly seems possible. Possible enough to affect my prayers. Now, when I pray, I can imagine the mechanism he can use to answer. How hard can it be, Lord, for you to change the energy level of that electron so that that molecule is weakened and that reaction between molecules is changed so that healing can happen?

Unfortunately, that leaves the question of why God does not heal all diseases nor make his sun to shine whenever it suits my fancy. But, we leave those questions for a different time and book. For now, it is enough to say that God can act if he so chooses. That alone can make a great difference in our prayers.

A God closer than imagined

Thinking on these things has quite significantly changed my picture of what is real. This stand-up desk is real, as is the back pain, my wife painting the walls in the next room, the sun streaming in my window and the noise from construction across the street. Yet, none of it is real in the way we have understood it to be. Particles exist in fields of indeterminate location, energy and matter are one and the same, and we are told that instead of just three dimensions of space and one of time we live in as many as ten dimensions. Particles once entangled stay that way and a change in one affects the other even across the universe. Most of what constitutes our universe in energy and matter is mysterious, unobservable, dark. And everything that appears solid and substantial is filled with vast areas of nothingness. I don't fall through the chair, the floor, the ground, the earth because of one thing -- the Pauli Exclusion Principle that simply says some particles are not allowed to occupy the same space/time as others. But, the space between an electron and its nucleus is immense. A common analogy of an atom has the nucleus as a fly in the center of a large sports arena with its electrons as tiny gnats circling the stadium. Since you and I are made up entirely of such atoms, that means we are almost entirely empty space. There's not much to us, so to speak. As a reminder of this view of reality I often picture a person or object I see as a cloud, a vaporous mist of tiny particles somehow barely connected. Sort of like the mass of dunlins, small seabirds that fly in a large flock with amazing speed, flitting back and forth over the landscape as if controlled by a single brain. And I wonder: God gave me eyes to see things as substantial and solid. What if I had new eyes to see things as they really were? C. S. Lewis' thought, in *The Great Divorce*, about heaven being of far greater substance than anything we know on earth might prove to be more than just fantasy.

But, is that space within us really empty? Where is God in all of this vast emptiness of our universe, our living spaces, our bodies? I can't say for certain where he is, but I do know that there's plenty of room within my very atoms for him to visit, if not live. That's the way I choose to envision God. All who think about God, atheist or theist alike, do at least some envisioning. Sure, the old man with the flowing white beard walking around on the clouds or inside a jeweled gate still constitutes a preferred image for many. Michelangelo did much to create a mental image of God with his arm reaching out to a newly created Adam in the Sistine Chapel. But that is a God-picture that has him farther away than I choose to imagine. In my choice of images, he is closer than my breath, closer than my heart, closer to me it seems than I am to myself. I now know that I in reality am nothing but a nearly empty cloud. Can a cloud fit within a cloud? Can smoke be added to smoke? Isn't it interesting then that the Person of the Godhead who is assigned to be with us is called "ruach" in Hebrew? Holy Spirit, Holy Ghost, Holy Smoke.

A God and world of freedom

Evolution has become the unfortunate dividing line between those supposedly faithful to the historic biblical faith and the new followers of the cult of science. Unfortunate, because this false conflict has hurt both the cause of science and the cause of faith. I stand firmly with those who accept that the process of evolution is a well-established scientific fact. It's called a theory but that does not make it untrue. Changes in the incredibly complex genetic code occur regularly. Most of those changes are damaging to the organism. Some are helpful in that they increase the chances of survival in a rough and tumble world. Because the strong, healthy and handsome survivors have the best and longest reproductive chances, those genetic changes are passed on to the next generation. That strikes me as being very well established and an absolutely brilliant way for the created world to make itself.

Note that I did not claim in accepting the truth of evolution that evolution provides a final and complete explanation. A few loud science writers make this claim. Most are more humble and honest than that. I did not claim that the beginning of life can be explained this way, nor even that this process explains the diversity of life, speciation and the emergence of a sentient, conscious organism we call human. It may be, but these things are not universally accepted by the scientific community.

Given the evidence we are presented today, it seems to me the most rational position we can take is directed evolution. God created the process by which the world largely makes itself. But he is also intimately involved in that continuing process and has created the means by which he can influence, if not manage, it without any violation of the laws so necessary to make it work. Polkinghorne describes directed evolution as water running down a hillside. There are many ways for the water to descend but the channels that are carved into the hillside provide a predictable path for the water to normally flow.

My own preference for the "how" of God's involvement in the continuing creation process is the same as the process he can use to answer your and my prayers: through chaos and uncertainty. I said that changes in the genetic code are what cause organisms to change and adapt to their environment. Scientists would declare that these changes are random. Perhaps. Perhaps almost all of them are. But once again, if God were to tweak this quark and touch that boson, would those observant scientists be able to definitely state that the resulting change in the particle was not random? I don't see how. All the changes, God-induced or not, would appear random. In such a way God can create the laws that are fixed and necessary, use chance as a self-creating engine, but still play an active guiding role without any violation.

I have thought much about the idea, so elegantly suggested by Polkinghorne, for the evidence that God makes a world that makes itself. Suppose that he does not involve himself to the degree that I suggested but rather it is in carving out the valleys and canyons that he knew would at some point in time result in a creature with whom he could enter into relationship. A world that makes itself is at one time frightening and magnificent. In some respects it shouts the glory of the Creator in new and unexpected ways. If God has granted the world such freedom, how much more has he granted us who have at least some understanding of our responsibility and the consequences of our actions. The gene in the DNA of the bird in the Galapagos did not think about the consequences of changing so that the beak of the bird carrying that gene will grow a bit odd but more capable of shelling the seeds of the island. The bird thinks no such thoughts either. But we are aware, usually, that what we do to others, to our world, to our children, to those around us, can have significant consequences for others, for all time. We do not need the movie *It's a Wonderful Life* to remind us that even the little ways in which we deal with others can change history.

Sometimes I fantasize that the world has some level of awareness of itself. That it is moving toward that day, when the groaning of the whole universe will end, and it will present itself in the Court of the Great King who gave it life, purpose, opportunity and freedom. And it will open its gown spreading out all the stars, all the planets, all the moons and the wondrous life on this planet and perhaps others and say, "See, this is what I did with the freedom you granted." And then I think about the planet, and stars, the cloud of being that constitutes myself. I do have awareness, not only of myself but of the Creator and his expectations and freedom. I will stand with the world in that Court, but what will I present? Every thought, every action, every choice that is truly mine will be the gift I have to display. What am I doing today with that freedom? What choices am I making with the particles I control with my consciousness? Will I be able to present them fearlessly and with joy to the Giver of All? I have been granted a kind of freedom that when I am confronted with the immensity of it can only bring me to my knees.

A God of information

As I write this, early in 2014, a new book has just come out by Max Tegmark, a highly regarded scientist from MIT. In it, *Our Mathematical Universe*, he makes the claim that not only does our world contain mathematics, but that it actually is made of mathematics. I admit, math was my worst subject in school and I know nothing of math, but it's a bit hard for me to think of this world as nothing more than some kind of abstract construct. Tegmark, like many of today's scientists writing for popular audiences, has strayed beyond traditional science, beyond the empirical and testable, into philosophy, theology and metaphysics. But, one thing seems certain about this world, information is real and it matters.

Our ability in this early part of the 21st century to translate a great deal of our reality into transferable information has transformed our lives and our world. Everything, these days, seems to be about ones and zeros and the machines that encode, store, work with and convey those two numbers. The reality we are able to reduce to these two numbers and manipulate with our machines is increasingly complex. It used to be numbers and words that were coded, now it is moving images, incredibly rich music and all the world's books. I sit out here in the California desert writing on a "pad" smaller and far lighter than most books in my library, yet from here in mere seconds I can access virtually all the knowledge and information created in almost ten thousand years of human history. Try to explain that to your great great grandfather.

We have also discovered that the engines of life run on code. These are chemical codes, but your and my DNA stores every last bit of the uniqueness of who we are in combinations of just four elements. It is now conceivable that every cell, every molecule, every atom, every particle could be enumerated in code, in numbers, even in sequences of zeroes and ones. There is nothing unique about the particles, atoms or molecules that constitute you and all your memories. We are all made up of stardust, the remains of exploding stars millions or billions of years ago. And the constituent parts are in constant change so that every seven years there is an entirely new you. Yet, you remain yourself, who you are, because what matters is not the constituent parts but how they are arranged and the relationship they have to each other. That is what makes you you--and that can be encoded. That can be understood as numbers. We are, ultimately it seems, information.

There is nothing that I have come across in this meandering journey I have shared with you that is more profound to me than that. I do not believe information is lost. I despaired a few years ago as the reality of aging pushed itself into my reflection and I considered that all I had learned, all I had read, all my experiences, all my memories were just patterns of interactions between nerve cells in my brain. Whether I lost control over those patterns through dementia or Alzheimer's disease or through death, when they were lost, I would be lost. Gone forever. It frightened me to think of being a living, sentient being experiencing the continual loss of all that made me who I am. But, I am information and you are information. Our true selves are not contained in the hardware of the computer of meat we carry on our necks. Our true selves, which of necessity include our unique experiences and memories, exist outside of that computer -- in the cloud. A concept much easier for us to accept and understand as we move all our data and operating software into "the cloud," that amorphous, vast interconnection of processing power distributed anywhere and everywhere. I firmly believe that our information is not lost but is maintained, even while operating in this frail, old processor, in the Cloud that is the mind of God.

Two things really matter as I contemplate the immortality of information. One is that immortality and the ancient Christian belief of resurrection takes on a new meaning and a new hope. As Polkinghorne and N.T. Wright both explain, our future is a hardware upgrade. The software we are given, that is our operating system and the data we collect and build through our lives, is not lost but preserved until that time when reinstalled in hardware that will never again need upgrading. My hope and confidence in that reality has grown in power and joy as the pieces fit together. One universal human experience is the sense that this is not all there is, that death is not the final act, that we are made for a world much greater than this. That universal intuition, combined with the remarkable historical fact that there was one human who, in full view of witnesses, had his hardware cruelly destroyed. But then, to the amazement of his friends and family, and to the continuing amazement of two billion of the world's souls, that destroyed hardware was replaced with a model with unbelievable new functionality. Then he, operating with this new processor, promised that the new generation hardware that was his reconstituted body was the same as what we could receive. Our destiny is not to die like dogs. Every part of our human intuition rebels against that thought. From the earliest days of human consciousness we have sensed that death is not the end. Now science seems to make it increasingly clear that we are not just a random collection of stardust, but that we are information that cannot be lost. Information that requires a body, hardware, substance in order to interact and relate to others and our creator -- exactly what has been promised to us in the ancient scripture.

The second thing that matters is that we are accountable for our information. If the world was set free to make itself, then we are as well. And if we are ultimately information, a recordable, transferable pattern, over which we exercise near dictatorial control then we are responsible for that information. What I take in matters not just to me now, but for all time and all eternity. If it is true that my memories remain because without them I lose who I really am, I am responsible for those memories. Surely a merciful God will free me from those memories that would otherwise torment me. But I cannot be given the data of another simply because I squandered my opportunity to create the information that I could value for all time and eternity. My information matters, now and always, and what I do to create, manage, store and process that is the essence of who I am and will be forever.

A God for all time and beyond

I just said the word "forever." I've talked of eternity, of time beyond time. Time is a mystery. It is a dimension of our reality, the fourth dimension. We live in three dimensions of space and one of time, but Einstein made clear that there is no real distinction between time and space. They were created together. Time started 13.7 billion years ago. Most of us still live in a world conceived of as dependent on fixed time while in reality we know that time is not fixed. Time to one human is not necessarily the same to another human being traveling at great speeds toward or away from us. I can't profess to understand any of it. I just know that soon it will once again be dinner time and after that, bedtime.

I can best understand the great limitations of our own experience of time by watching a hummingbird zip at what seems to me supersonic speeds as it gathers nectar. I flinch when they fly so close to my head thinking how can they see me that quickly to miss? Yet, what a silly thing for a hummingbird. I imagine he looks at me and sees me as a mountain or iceberg moving mere inches in his years. A single keystroke here and he would complete hundreds of wingbeats and find a whole new delicious source of nutrition in my bougainvillea.

We tend to think of eternity as a long, long, long time. The Psalmist said a thousand years to God is as a day, but the Psalmist was poetic and wrong, I think. If God is as what we think (and I'm sure he is not, but we still need to talk about it) then he is in time and bound by its requirements while still being completely outside of it. That is an antonym but no greater than the antonym of the Trinity or most of our other beliefs about God. Outside of time, time has no meaning. As C.S. Lewis believed, God lives in an eternal now. What happened the Valley of Elah about 3000 years ago as a young boy faced a mighty warrior is happening right now in the same way that the moment of my death is happening right now. All is now. Yesterday, today and tomorrow are all included in now. Now is all.

Long ago, I can't say whom I learned it from exactly, but I came to understand that the secret of contentment and peace was living in now. Not yesterday with its sorrows and regrets, not tomorrow with its false hopes and fears, but now. Because in all but the most extreme circumstances such as hunger, fire, bullets flying or other imminent danger, we can say truthfully now is OK. If I just look at now, it is good. In fact, usually in that OK and with a release of all cares and worries and thoughts about yesterday or tomorrow the now is quickly flooded with an inexpressible joy. I have come that you might have life in all its abundance, we are told by God. All that life in its abundance is and can only be found in now. Everything else is illusion. And now is the natural and everlasting home of God.

A God who wants to be known

Can science contribute anything to the idea of a God who desires a real, direct, intimate and personal relationship with his creatures? That may seem the silliest of all ideas in this book. But let me suggest two ways that turn out to be one: mathematics and beauty.

Search the bookshelves, virtually if you must, for contemporary writings about cosmology, physics and quantum mechanics. You will find an inordinate number dealing with mathematics and reality. Is God a mathematician? one asks. Another suggests that math is the only reality--everything else is illusion. But one strain remains consistent: the sheer mystery of the universe's comprehensibility through math. Why should this be so? Why should first of all it be constituted in such a way that abstract constructs such as $E=MC^2$ would so wonderfully describe it? And how can it be that a completely naturalistic world should result in conscious, intelligent creatures which are able to create a language that has the unique power to unlock the mysteries of the universe? For those of you who find the idea of God so troubling, but yet have found your knees buckle when confronted with the profound revelations of mathematics, I ask you, where does that sense of wonder come from?

I am making the simple suggestion that math, though it be a human created language, is one of the most compelling pieces of evidence that the mind of the creator wishes to be known.

I am far more artist than I am mathematician. When artist types like me talk about beauty it is about aesthetics, about magnificent paintings, sculpture, music, dance or architecture. So when I read about physicists enthusing about the "beauty" of a formula or even more, decide on the truth of a mathematical solution based on its elegance, I wonder if we are talking about the same concept of beauty. Now I absolutely believe we are. Umberto Eco, in his book *Art and Beauty in the Middle Ages* said "the aesthetic impulse arises when the soul finds its inner harmony duplicated in its object." The soul's inner harmony duplicated in its object. Simple words that describe a reality that is at the heart of who we are as humans, that illuminate an experience that surely all who are capable of overwhelming feelings at the sight of the truly beautiful have enjoyed. But, where does this inner harmony come from? How can it be that there arises in us a sense of rightness, perfection, exuberance that is found in the deepest recesses of who we are but which can be brought forth into the chemicals and synapses of our brains when confronted with an object of intense beauty? Is it really rational to think that such a thing is a quite natural result of some genetic mutation and that this most universal and profound of human experiences describes a survival advantage?

We know that at the heart of this world there is a deep connection between beauty and truth. Perhaps, as Keats suggested, they are in reality the same. He further suggested that that connection was all we knew and all we could know. For all we have learned of this natural created world, for all our data, all our knowledge, all our insight into the true nature of what we experience as reality, I'm not certain that Keats is far from the truth. For at bottom the beauty and the truth is this: God is and God is love.

Notes

Chapter 1   Dissonance: Of Two Minds

1. (Wikipedia) Darwin, C. R. 1958. The autobiography of Charles Darwin 1809-1882. With the original omissions restored. Edited with appendix and notes by his grand-daughter Nora Barlow. London: Collins, p. 87

Chapter 2   Isms: Is God There?

1. Nahum M. Sarna, Book of Psalms: Exploring the Prayers of Ancient Israel, Nahum M. Sarna, Schocken Books, New York, 1993, p. 6

2. John Polkinghorne, *Quarks, Chaos & Christianity: Questions to Science and Religion*, p. 36

3. Tiner, J.H. (1975). *Isaac Newton: Inventor, Scientist and Teacher.* Milford, Michigan, U.S.: Mott Media.

4. Stephen W. Hawking, *A Brief History of Time*, p. 174

5. http://www.reasons.org/fine-tuning-life-universe

6. Ibid., p. 122

7. Ibid., p. 125

8. Ibid., p. 124-125

9. Stephen M. Barr, *Modern Physics and Ancient Faith,*, University of Notre Dame, p. 130

10. John Polkinghorne, *Science and Theology*, p. 75-76

11. Barr, p. 157

Chapter 3   Quantum World: A Very Strange Place

1. http://en.wikipedia.org/wiki/Quantum_entanglement

2. Polkinghorne, *Quarks, Chaos and Christianity*, p. 70-71

3. http://en.wikipedia.org/wiki/Quantum_entanglement

4. http://en.wikipedia.org/wiki/Dark_matter (Aug 2009)

5. Stephen Hawking, *Universe in a Nutshell*, p. 139

Chapter 4   Chaos: Butterflies, Golf and Miracles

1. John Barrow, *New Theories of Everything*, p. 63

2. John Barrow, *New Theories of Everything*, p. 63

3. John Barrow, *New Theories of Everything*, p. 65

3. John Conway, Princeton Lecture, Free Will Theorem, March 2009
https://www.princeton.edu/main/news/archive/S23/75/58A30/index.xml?section=featured

Chapter 5   Evolution: Whale Hands and a World That Makes Itself

1. Charles Darwin, *Origin of the Species*, p. 48

2. James Weldon Johnson, The Creation
http://www.poetry-archive.com/j/the_creation.html

3. David Lindley, *The End of Physics: The Myth of a Unified Theory*, p. 131

4. Francis Collins, *The Language of God*, p. 90

5. Francis Collins, *The Language of God*, p. 93

6. . Blogpost on BioLogos Foundation website, October 16, 2009 by Shelly Emling, author of The Fossil Hunter.
http://biologos.org/blog/finding-common-ground

"Simon Conway-Morris, the renowned paleontologist at Cambridge University, is just one scientist who argues that religion and science are completely compatible. The British professor believes evolution isn't as accidental or random as one might suspect. In his opinion, if evolution began all over again, human intelligence would develop pretty much in the same way as it has. Conway-Morris emphasizes that developments happen as a result of pre-existing conditions, such as the need for blood cells to have hemoglobin in order to transport oxygen. Evolution, therefore, works only because it plays out within a certain set of rules.

Evolution "is after all only a mechanism, but if evolution is predictive, indeed possesses a logic, then evidently it is being governed by deeper principles," he recently wrote. "Come to think about it so are all sciences; why should Darwinism be any exception?"

Chapter 6: Information: Foundation and Immortality

Chapter 7: Observation: Why Consciousness is Real and Necessary

1. p. 81 Richard Feynman, quote variously attributed: reference: http://blogs.discovermagazine.com/cosmicvariance/2011/02/15/is-relativity-hard/#.U5d10JSwKe0

2. Isaac Newton on light, http://en.wikipedia.org/wiki/Light,

3. Bruce Rosenblum and Fred Kuttner, *Quantum Enigma*, pps. 5, 203, 184

4. Jim Baggott's 2013 book *Farewell to Reality: How Modern Physics Has Betrayed the Search for Scientific Truth,* location 94

Chapter 8   Authority: Who Owns the Truth

Dr. Hugh Ross, Reasons to Believe: http://www.reasons.org/articles/defending-concordism-response-to-the-lost-world-of-genesis-one)

Chapter 9   Legacy: On the Shoulder of Giants

1. Plato quotation: https://librivox.org/phaedrus-by-plato

2. Mark A. Noll, Galileo quotation, *Jesus Christ and the Life of the Mind*, location 1172

3. Alister McGrath, quoting Maimonides, *Science and Religion: A New Introduction*, location 3137

4. Isaac Newton, quotes from the text, *Memoirs of the Life, Writings, and discoveries of Sir Isaac Newton, volume 2* by Sir David Brewster from 1855 and available in full on Google Books. Page 450.

5. Noll, on Augustine's "disgraceful and dangerous" in *Jesus Christ and the Life of the Mind*, location 1131 (quoted from St Augustine, "The Literal Meaning of Genesis" translated by John Hammond Taylor, S.J 1:42-43)

Chapter 10   Metaphysic: Spiritual and Material Realities

1. *Consciousness After Death: Strange Tales From the Frontiers of Resuscitation Medicine*
By Brandon Keim, Wired Magazine, April 24, 2013

Parnia: When you die, there's no blood flow going into your brain. If it goes below a certain level, you can't have electrical activity. It takes a lot of imagination to think there's somehow a hidden area of your brain that comes into action when everything else isn't working.

These observations raise a question about our current concept of how brain and mind interact. The historical idea is that electrochemical processes in the brain lead to consciousness. That may no longer be correct, because we can demonstrate that those processes don't go on after death. There may be something in the brain we haven't discovered that accounts for consciousness, or it may be that consciousness is a separate entity from the brain.

Wired: This seems to verge on supernatural explanations of consciousness.

Parnia: Throughout history, we try to explain things the best we can with the tools of science. But most open-minded and objective scientists recognize that we have limitations. Just because something is inexplicable with our current science doesn't make it superstitious or wrong. When people discovered electromagnetism, forces that couldn't then be seen or measured, a lot of scientists made fun of it. Scientists have come to believe that the self is brain cell processes, but there's never been an experiment to show how cells in the brain could possibly lead to human thought. If you look at a brain cell under a microscope, and I tell you, "this brain cell thinks I'm hungry," that's impossible.

2.   Alan Guth, on the origins using quantum fluctuations and inflation: (quoted in Nichols' *Sacred Cosmos*, p. 76

3. Alan Lightman, *The Accidental Universe,* p. 12, location 154

4. Cox, Brian; Forshaw, Jeff (2011). *The Quantum Universe : Everything That Can Happen Does Happen*

5. Alan Lightman, The Accidental Universe, p. 21, location 246

6. Jim Baggott, *Farewell to Reality: How Modern Science Has Betrayed the Search for Scientific Truth*, Location 4073

7. Marcelo Gleiser, NPR blog, November 28, 2012
http://www.npr.org/blogs/13.7/2012/11/28/165993001/astrotheology-do-gods-need-to-be-supernatural

Chapter 11   Theology: What Difference Does it Make?

Bibliography

Armstrong, Karen, (2009). *The Case for God,* Alfred A. Knopf/Random House: New York

Armstrong, Karen, (1996). *In the Beginning: A New Interpretation of Genesis,* Ballantine/Random House: New York

Aczel, Amir, (2014). *Why Science Does Not Disprove God,* HarperCollins: New York

Baggott, Jim. (2013). *Farewell to Reality: How Modern Physics Has Betrayed the Search for Scientific Truth,* Pegasus: New York

Barr, Stephen M., (2003). *Modern Physics and Ancient Faith,* University of Notre Dame Press: Notre Dame, IN

Barrow, John D., (2007). *New Theories of Everything: The Quest for Ultimate Explanation,* Oxford University Press: Oxford

Bohm, David, (1951). *Quantum Theory,* Dover: New York

Brockman, John, editor, (2006). *What We Believe But Cannot Prove: Today's Leading Thinkers on Science in the Age of Certainty,* Harper Collins: New York

Brooke, John & Geoffrey Cantor, (1998). *Reconstructing Nature: The Engagement of Science and Religion,* Oxford University Press: Oxford

Butchins, Adair, (2002). *The Numinous Legacy: Modern Cosmology and Religion,* Albatross Press, UK

Cole, K.C., (2003). *Mind Over Matter: Conversations with the Cosmos,* Harcourt: Orlando, Florida

Coles, Peter, (2001). *Cosmology: A Very Short Introduction*, Oxford University Press: Oxford

Cox, Brian and Forshaw, Jeff, (2009). *Why Does E=MC²: And Why Should We Care?*, DaCapo Press: Cambridge, MA

Cox, Brian and Cohen, Andrew, (2011). *Wonders of the Universe*, Harper Collins: New York

Cox, Brian and Forshaw, Jeff, (2011). The Quantum Universe (And Why Anything That Can Happen, Does), DaCapo Press: Cambridge, MA

Collins, Francis S., (2006). *The Language of God: A Scientist Presents Evidence for Belief,* Free Press: London

Collins, John C., (2011). *Did Adam and Eve Ever Exist? Who They Were and Why You Should Care*, Crossway: Wheaton, IL

Craig, William Lane, (2010). *On Guard: Defending Your Faith with Reason and Precision,* David C. Cook: Colorado Springs, Colorado

Davies, Paul, (1992). *The Mind of God: Scientific Basis for a Rational World,* Simon & Schuster: New York

Davies, Paul, (1999). *The 5th Miracle: The Search for the Origin and Meaning of Life,* Touchstone: New York

Dennett, Daniel C., (2006). *Breaking the Spell: Religion as a Natural Phenomenon*, Penguin: New York

D'Souza, Dinesh, (2009). *Life After Death: The Evidence*, Regnery Publishing: Washington DC

Dyson, Freeman, editor, (2010) *The Best American Science and Nature Writing 2010*, Houghton Mifflin Harcourt: New York

Eisley, Loren, (1978). *The Star Thrower*, Harcourt Brace & Company: San Diego

Eisley, Loren, (1964). *The Unexpected Universe*, Harvest/HBJ: New York

Enns, Peter, (2012). *The Evolution of Adam: What the Bible Does and Doesn't Say About Human Origins*, Brazos Press/ Baker: Grand Rapids, MI

Ferris, Timothy, (1997). *The Whole Shebang: A State-of-the-Universe(s) Report,* Simon & Schuster: New York

Feynman, Richard P. and Leighton, Ralph, (1985). *Surely You're Joking Mr. Feynman!: Adventures of a Curious Character*, W.W. Norton: New York

Flew, Anthony with Roy Abraham Varghese. (2007) *There is A God: How the World's Most Notorious Atheist Changed His Mind,* HarperCollins: New York

Frenkel, Edwin, (2013). *Love and Math: The Heart of Hidden Reality,* Basic/Perseus: Philadelphia

Gilson, Tom and Weitnauer, Carson, editors, (2012) *True Reason: Christian Responses to the Challenge of Atheism,* Patheos Press: Englewood, Colorado

Green, Michael, (2013) *Quantum Physics and Ultimate Reality: Mystical Writings of Great Physicists*, Amazon Kindle Direct: Seattle, WA

Haarsma, Deborah B. and Haarsma, Loren D., (2011). *Origins: Christian Perspectives on Creation, Evolution, and Intelligent Design*, Faith Alive: Grand Rapids, MI

Hawking, Stephen, (1988). *A Brief History of Time: From the Big Bang to Black Holes,* Bantam: New York

Hawking, Stephen & Mlodinow, Leonard, (2010). *The Grand Design*, Bantam: New York

Hawking, Stephen, (2001). *The Universe in a Nutshell*, Bantam: New York

Holt, Jim, (2012). *Why Does the World Exist?: An Existential Detective Story*, Liveright/W.W. Norton: New York

Kaku, Michio, (2008) *Physics of the Impossible: A Scientific Exploration Into the World of Phasers, Force Fields, Teleportation, and Time Travel,* Random House: New York

Kurten, Bjorn, (1984). Not From the Apes: A History of Man's Origins and Evolution, Columbia University Press: New York

Kurzweil, Ray, (2012). *How to Create a Mind: The Secret of Human Thought Revealed,* Viking/Penguin: New York

Leslie, John, (2007). *Immortality Defended*, Blackwell: Malden, MA

Leslie, John, (1989). *Universes,* Routledge: London

Lindley, David, (1993). *The End of Physics: The Myth of a Unified Theory,* Basic/HarperCollins: New York

Lightman, Alan, (2013). *The Accidental Universe: The World You Thought You Knew,* Pantheon: Toronto, Canada

Lineweaver, Charles H.; Davies, Paul C.; Ruse, Michael, editors, (2013). *Complexity and the Arrow of Time*, Cambridge University Press, Cambridge, UK

Livio, Mario, (2009). *Is God a Mathematician?*, Simon & Schuster: New York

Loconte, Joseph, (2012). *The Searchers: A Quest for Faith in the Valley of Doubt,* Thomas Nelson: Nashville, Tennessee

McGrath, Alister, (2004). *The Science of God: An Introduction to Scientific Theology,* Wm B. Eerdmans, Grand Rapids, MI

McGrath, Alister, (2006). *The Twilight of Atheism: The Rise and Fall of Disbelief in the Modern World,* Doubleday/Random House: New York

McGrath, Alister, (2007). *Dawkins' God: Genes, Memes, and the Meaning of Life,* Blackwell Publishing: Oxford

McGrath, Alister, (2010). *Science & Religion: A New Introduction, Second Edition,* Wiley-Blackwell: Chichester, UK

Medina, John, (2008). *Brain Rules: 12 Principles for Surviving and Thriving at Work, Home and School*, Pear Press: Seattle, WA

Miller, James W., (2013). *Hardwired: Finding the God You Already Know,* Abingdon Press: Nashville, Tennessee

Miller, Kenneth R., (1999). *Finding Darwin's God: A Scientist's Search for Common Ground Between God and Evolution,* HarperCollins: New York

Mlodinow, Leonard, (2003). *Feynman's Rainbow: A Search for Beauty in Physics and in Life,* Warner Books: New York

Morris, Henry M. & John D., (1996). *The Modern Creation Trilogy: Scripture & Creation, Volume One,* Master Books: Green Forest, AR

Nagel, Thomas, (2012). *Mind and Cosmos: Why the Materialist Neo-Darwinian Conception of Nature of Almost Certainly False*, Oxford University Press: Oxford

Nicholi, Dr. Armand M., Jr., (2002). *The Question of God: C.S. Lewis and Sigmund Freud Debate God, Love, Sex, and the Meaning of Life,* Free Press/Simon & Schuster: New York

Nichols, Terence L., (2003). *The Sacred Cosmos: Christian Faith and the Challenge of Naturalism*, Baker Book House: Grand Rapids, MI

Noll, Mark A., (2011). *Jesus Christ and the Life of the Mind*, Eerdmans: Grand Rapids, MI

Padamsee, Hasan S., (2003). *Unifying the Universe: The Physics of Heaven and Earth,* Institute of Physics Publishing: Bristol and Philadelphia

Plantinga, Alvin, (2011). *Where the Conflict Really Lies: Science, Religion and Naturalism,* Oxford University Press: New York

Polkinghorne, John C., (1998). *Belief in God in an Age of Science*, Yale University Press: New Haven, London

Polkinghorne, John C., (2005). *Science and Providence: God's Interaction with the World,* Templeton Foundation Press: West Conshohocken, PA

Polkinghorne, John C., (1998). *Science and Theology: An Introduction,* SPCK/Fortress Press: London

Polkinghorne, John C., (2002). *Quantum Theory: A Very Short Introduction*, Oxford University Press: Oxford

Polkinghorne, John C. & Nicholas Beale, (2009). *Questions of Truth: Fifty-one Responses to Questions about God, Science and Belief*, Westminster John Knox Press: Louisville, KY

Polkinghorne, John C., (2007) *Quantum Physics and Theology: An Unexpected Kinship,* Yale University Press: New Haven

Polkinghorne, John, (1998). *Science and Theology: An Introduction,* SPCK/Fortress Press: London

Polkinghorne, John C., (1996). *The Faith of a Physicist: Reflections of a Bottom-Up Thinker,* Fortress Press: Minneapolis, MN

Polkinghorne, John C., (1994). *Quarks, Chaos & Christianity,* Crossroad Publishing: New York

Randall, Lisa. (2011), *Knocking on Heaven's Door: How Physics and Scientific Thinking Illuminate the Universe and the Modern World,* Harper Collins: New York

Randall, Lisa, (2013). *Higgs Discovery: The Power of Empty Space,* Harper Collins: New York

Rau, Gerald, (2012). *Mapping the Origins Debate: Six Models of the Beginning of Everything,* Intervarsity Press: Downers Grove, IL

Rosenblum, Bruce and Kuttner, Fred, (2006). *Quantum Enigma: Physics Encounters Consciousness,* Oxford University Press: New York

Ross, Hugh, (2010). *Beyond the Cosmos: What Recent Discoveries in Astrophysics Reveal About the Glory and Love of God, Third Edition,* Reasons to Believe: Glendora, California

Sarna, Nahum M., (1993). *Book of Psalms: Exploring the Prayers of Ancient Israel,* Schocken Books: New York

Schroeder, Gerald L., (1990). *Genesis and the Big Bang: The Discovery of Harmony Between Modern Science and the Bible,* Bantam Books: New York

Thomas, Lewis, (1974). *The Lives of a Cell: Notes of a Biology Watcher,* Bantam Books: Toronto

Swinburne, Richard, (2003) *Is There A God?,* Oxford University Press: Oxford

Walton, John H., (2006). *Ancient Near Eastern Thought and the Old Testament: Introducing the Conceptual World of the Hebrew Bible,* Baker Academic: Grand Rapids, MI

Walton, John H., (2009). *The Lost World of Genesis One: Ancient Cosmology and the Origins Debate,* Intervarsity Press: Downers Grove, IL

Ward, Keith, (2007). *Rethinking Christianity,* Oneworld: Oxford

Ward, Keith, (2008). *Why There Almost Certainly Is a God: Doubting Dawkins,* Lion Hudson: Oxford

Wilson, John, (1885). *Thoughts on Science, Theology And Ethics,* Trubner & Company, Ludgate Hill: London

Wright, Robert, (2009). *The Evolution of God,* Little, Brown & Company: New York

Wright, N.T., (2008), *Surprised by Hope: Rethinking Heaven, the Resurrection, and the Mission of the Church,* Harper Collins, New York

www.ingramcontent.com/pod-product-compliance
Lightning Source LLC
LaVergne TN
LVHW051404080426
835508LV00022B/2976